AN EVENIN
Murder Mystery Plays

Plays to be performed for Comedy Dinner Theater

By David J. Fielding

Copyright © 2013

So, you want to know Whodunnit?

Well, let's see if we can't help you figure it out, shall we?

My name is David J. Fielding and I am an actor and writer. My most notable claim to fame is as the character of Zordon on the original **Migthy Morphin' Power Rangers** television series. For the last thirty years of my life I have made a living as an actor, writer and game designer. My real passion is writing and that's the real reason behind this book of plays, to share with you some of the shows I have written and some of my experience about doing murder mystery dinner theater.

My introduction to Murder Mystery Comedy Theater came a bit late, after two college degrees, a stint living and acting in Los Angeles and making a living as an actor in the city of Pittsburgh, PA. I was introduced to a fellow actor and performer who ran a company that provided the shows and actors for a dinner theater at a local restaurant – they were looking to replace a member and after seeing me perform and talking for a bit, I was hired. I didn't really know what I was getting into at the time, but in hindsight, it turned out to be a very good thing – and the memories and friends I've made through this type of theater have been some the best in my life.

Dinner Theater has been around for a very long time – since the Middle Ages in fact (if not before that - as my first script indicates – just a bit of shameless self-promotion there). Groups of players and musicians would be hired to perform for nobles or royalty while they enjoyed a sumptuous meal.

Today, Dinner Theater is still drawing crowds and giving patrons a night's worth of entertainment for little cost. Generally, the dining area and the stage area are separated as they would be in a regular theater, the stage upfront for all to see, and the tables arranged where the normal seating would be located.

But what makes many Murder Mystery shows truly entertaining is the aspect of audience interaction. Most murder mystery dinner theater – at least the kind I am most familiar with – takes place in the dining area itself, with the audience smack dab in the middle of the action.

We all love a mystery. We all like solving riddles and unraveling clues and getting those "A-ha!" moments of discovery – when we see the pieces fall into place and we figure out what happened. What makes those moments even more enjoyable is doing so with friends or with a group that is attempting to figure out the mystery together.

One of the wonderful things about murder mystery dinner theater is that it is not something anyone takes seriously.

Now, don't get me wrong – the work that goes into putting together a murder mystery dinner is demanding and there are a lot of dedicated people the world round who devote a lot of hours into making ***good*** dinner theater. I'm not going to go into detail about what is good or bad dinner theater – you know them when you see them.

What I mean by not taking it seriously is that the immediacy of the audience to the actors and action of the play lend itself to comedy more readily than melodrama or serious theater. The tropes of the types of plays that are performed – fake pistols, fake blood, fake cleavage (we'll get to that) are all to easily seen through by the audience when it takes place mere feet from you. And because we can see through the fakery, it creates a lighter mood – one where both the audience and the actors have the freedom to laugh and interact.

But that is what makes doing this type of theater fun for both actor's and audience members – we are all in on the joke – it's a true shared experience.

The key to a truly exceptional murder mystery show is *interaction* – the more the better. In my personal experience, the more interactive the show, the more fun and enjoyment was had by all. By interaction I mean the give and take with the audience, those rare moments when an actor steps away from the scripted material and makes the moment one-of-kind, a personal moment between audience and character.

This is exactly the type of moment you want to happen during a murder mystery show – it breaks the fourth wall, and engages the audience. Some of the best moments that I have had on stage have been these type of unscripted or blooper moments – when the actors have to think on their feet and save the moment or drag it back even after it has fallen flat on its face. It's the same type of off-the-cuff, inspiration that you see during an improv show. Improv is a skill your actors need to be familiar with.

The interaction of your shows has to be driven by the actors, and the shows will live or die by their participation or lack thereof. I cannot stress to you enough the importance of hiring and working with actor's who are comfortable with this type of performance.

The type of actor or performer that shines at this type of show is the one that thrives on this type of interaction, and who is comfortable to wander – sometimes for several minutes – away from the scripted material and giving the show a one-of-kind feeling.

The camaraderie between the actors in the show cannot be overlooked – it isn't merely something you hope will happen, it is vital - it is so important to have other actors you can trust and enjoy performing with. The give and take between actors who know each other and the scripts well and that can make each other laugh helps to create moments that give the shows those priceless side-splitting moments of comedic gold.

Finding and working with these types of actors is a great way to keep your own talent evolving and improving. It also helps to make the shows you do together to stand head and shoulders above the rest of the dinner theater out there; the kind of experience that generates repeat business and allows you to perform this kind of show for fun and profit.

So, what is Murder Mystery Dinner Theater, exactly?

Well, at its core, it's a play that involves a number of shady characters who are brought together in a particular location and one of them ends up the victim of foul play. The rest of the play involves digging around for clues and motives, accusations between various characters' and the solving of the crime. The killer is brought to justice or gets his or her comeuppance and the rest of the player's exeunt happily ever after. The audience enjoys a fine meal and an evening's entertainment, and the actor's leave the venue, cackling wildly and counting the wads of cash and loot they were able to…

Oh, wait, no that last part doesn't really happen. Ok, once it happened, but it was only because a lot of the patrons were really drunk and just kept throw cash at us… no, no, I'm kidding. It never happens that way. Never.

Moving on.

This type of theater is normally run in cooperation with a restaurant of some sort, be it a chain restaurant or a family run establishment, where a package deal of dinner and a show makes the ticket affordable. But there are many companies that also travel with the shows to venue to venue or even to a private residence to perform the show for guests.

Typically, the guests will arrive at the location (restaurant, VFW Hall, community center, where have you) and find their seats at the tables in the dining space. On the tables, information about the upcoming show will be provided in a program – the program should include the title of the show and details about the setting and the characters. Patrons might also find clue sheets and a few golf pencils to write down info they gather during the performance.

The programs will generally include the title of the show, the setting and some brief background information about the show – for example:

"Murder in Morocco"
There's Some Dastardly Dirty Dealings going on at Slick Rick's Café!

Setting
1942, Morocco – Slick Rick's Café – April 14th, 7:45pm
It's a dangerous time to run a business what with the damn war going on, Nazi's poking their noses into everybody's business and now an old girlfriend shows up to throw a wrench into everything to boot! Some days it doesn't pay to get out of bed.

This would be followed by paragraphs that detail each of the characters in the play, along with a reason or two while they aren't to be trusted – for example:

Richard Matthews aka Rick
Rick is the suave and dashing owner of a nightclub that caters to the high and the low – it doesn't matter to Rick who drinks in his club, as long as their money is good. Rick doesn't talk much about his past – and with good reason. There's more than a few skeletons in his closet... and a few of those bony secrets are about to walk in his front door!

The program serves an important function because it's the first information the audience has regarding the show and also giving them clues that will appear later on in the show itself.

In addition, the programs may include a humorous clue or red herring about one of the characters. Audience members are encouraged to visit other tables to gather clues and to interact and share information with other people in the audience.

The Murder Mystery show does have a game show element to it – the audience is informed at the top that there will be prizes awarded to those who correctly guess the culprit of tonight's mystery.

It is therefore important that you also include a *Whodunnit* or *Detective Sheet* along with the Program. This is simply a piece of paper that includes a space for them to write down the name of the character they think is guilty, how they did it and why. Remember to leave a space for them to write their name down so that at the end of the show you can announce their name should they be picked as the winner. Have fun designing your Program and Who Done It Sheets; tailor them to the type of performance and time period of the play.

Ok, so we've talked about the set up a bit, now let's get into performance.

Due to the variety of playing spaces that a murder mystery company might find themselves in, it is necessary that the shows be tailored to fit any room they will be performed in. If possible, try to get to the space before the performance to check it out and to familiarize yourself with how the tables will be arranged. If possible, ask to have a space in the center of the room cleared so that a majority of the action can take place there, allowing the audience an unobstructed view of the action. Travel light - try to keep the costumes and props to a minimum and include enough room for a portable sound system.

Unlike traditional theater, there is no separation between the audience and the playing area – the cast is encouraged to play the show in between the dinner guests and tables, as well as the open space in the center. Remember, immediacy and interaction is what you are striving for – make the audience a participant in the show.

All companies operate differently – some prefer to start the show like a normal play – with the action starting from the top of the show. Others include a pre-show mingle.

A pre-show mingle involves the actors mingling with the audience in character, dropping hints and clues about the other characters and the setting and also involving the audience right from the very beginning.

As an actor it is your job to create the atmosphere of the show you are going to be performing. Interactions with the audience should be made in character and also allude to the time and setting of the play. If you are performing a play set in the 20's or 30's, during the audience mingle portion of the show, make references to the time period, styles of dress or events and famous people of the era.

Once the show begins it should be played in accordance with the arrangement worked out with the restaurant or dining venue – some venues like Acts I & II to run together, with the dessert being served before Act II; other venues like Act I and then dinner and then Act II followed by dessert. It really is up to the company and the venue to work out the running order.

Typically the diner guests will arrive to tables that have the necessary show and character information set beforehand. Their orders are taken or the buffet dinner served and during this portion of the evening, the pre-show mingle will occur, allowing the patrons to dine at a leisurely pace while also getting drawn into the show and getting to know the characters.

Once the dinner has been cleared then the show begins. After Act II is concluded, there is a short Q&A period with the audience, a final chance for them to gather clues and questions suspects before using the Whodunnit or Detective Sheets to write down their answers.

The Q&A should consist of four or five questions per character – actor's need to rely on the familiarity with the role and the script to answer questions, keeping the tone light and humorous.

Once the Q&A is finished the cast exists while dessert is served. After a few minutes the cast returns to collect the answer sheets and then to tally the winners' answers and to select the ones they feel best match the solution given in the play. Once the winners are chosen and the awards designated, the cast returns for the conclusion of the show, the reveal of the culprit and the wrap up.

The shows typically end with the introduction of the actors and the handing out the awards and a heartfelt and generous thank you to the audience and wait staff. Then it's time to clean up, pack up, count your winnings and move on to the next performance!

So, with a basic understanding of how the show is run, let's talk a bit about the plays included in this volume.

When I first began acting with the mystery theater we were given scripts that were fairly basic. And while they were funny, they didn't quite match the talent and energy our group soon discovered was really our strong point. We would lament after the shows that we wished we had better material to work with – and after one such evening, I asked if they wouldn't mind if I took a shot at writing a script for us. They agreed and I sat down to write one.

It was a lot of fun and I thoroughly enjoyed myself, especially when, during the read-through with the cast that they laughed at the right places and offered suggestions to firm up the characters and motivations. We produced it a few months later to great success and that show is still being played today.

As a note of interest, these scripts are presented without musical numbers – though it is quite common for shows of this type to include them. Songs are generally a fun bit for the cast an audience because it breaks up the action and adds a bit of variety to just a lot of information and clue gathering; plus it allows the more musically inclined members of the cast a chance to shine. They can also easily be added or removed from the script without causing a loss of important information necessary to the solving of the mystery. All of the songs you use in the scripts should be Karaoke versions with alternative lyrics which can be protected under the fair use and parody law.

Suggestions for songs to be used in the plays included in this volume are as follows:

The Roman Show - **JUMP, JIVE AND WAIL by Louie Prima** (*the Brian Setzer Orchestra version*) – this song can be inserted after EMPRESS CHIANTI's line: "And I know exactly how I want my first New Empire party to start --with decadence, debauchery and dancing!"

The Evil Genius Show – **I SAW HER SPYING THERE (I SAW HER STANDING THERE)** by Lennon/McCartney (*the Beatles version*) – this song can be inserted after ALEXIS VULVAE's line:

"And here all along I thought you were trying to foil my scheme to steal millions from the Stardust and MGM Grand…"

The Superhero Show – **4 MINUTES** by Madonna (*featuring Justin Timberlake & Timbaland*) – this song can be inserted after The COWL's line:
"The people of Gothamville adored OMEGAMAN… they're gonna want his killer's head on a plate!"

Obviously the lyrics of the songs should be tailored to fit the theme of the show – hence the lyrics to *I Saw Her Spying There* should follow the idea of the characters spying on one another, etc. Put your thinking caps on and work together to make them funny!

The following three scripts are shows that have yet to be produced, and are different than your typical 30's or 40's noir/detective murder mystery, English drawing room whodunit or 'Mr. Green, in the Dining Room, with the candlestick' send-up. They are presented as is and as examples of what an inventiveness, imagination and a healthy dose of humor can do to turn the typical murder mystery upside down and present a unique and fun show to the audience.

I hope you have as much fun reading them as I did writing them, and who knows, perhaps one day we'll put them up on their feet and see how many belly laughs we can get with them.

David J. Fielding
April 2013

The Tragic Life and Comic Death of Julius Iglesias Cincinnatus

or

SAY...ISN'T THAT YOUR DAGGER IN MY BACK?

By
David J. Fielding
Copyright © 2001

SETTING

All of the action of this Imperial Dastardly Comedy-Mystery, takes place in the Palace of the Emperor in the Glorious City of Rome, 276 A. C. E. at approximately 7:45pm on the evening of the Festival of the Cranky Virgin.

All the actors mingle in with the audience before the show begins, dropping hints, suggestions and innuendo about their pasts.

~~~~~~~~~~~~~~~~~~

CHARACTERS

JULIUS IGLESIAS CINCINNATUS
- the Emperor -- Dictator of Rome and all Her Provinces

Having served as Rome's Emperor for the last thirty years or so, some people believe that Julius is losing his grip on reality due to his advanced age -- there is evidence to support this as he continually refers to the Senate as "those cute Circus Performers" and has been insisting that his prize racing horse, Jack-of-all-Trades, be allowed to eat at the dinner table. His strange behavior and erratic antics have started the rumors flying that someday soon, if he isn't careful, someone might pull a Brutus on him -- and he just might find himself lying face down in a pool of his own gore on the steps of the Senate!

THE EMPRESS CHIANTI
- Wife of Julius, High Priestess of the Vestal Virgins and full time floozy

Empress Chianti spends most of her days entertaining visiting dignitaries at the Palace, lounging at the Roman Baths or arranging the occasional Orgy thrown by her organization: the Festival of the Month Club (South Side Chapter). She is very excited because tonight is the Festival of the Cranky Vestal Virgin, which means that there will be lots and lots of young studs for her to flirt and carouse with. The Empress is quite happy with her lot in life, except for one nagging detail - her husband. She feels he is too old for her and therefore cannot attend to her properly...for this reason she has started an illicit affair with the Emperor's ambitious younger brother, Tentacles. It is also rumored that Empress feels that the time is ripe for there to be a new Roman Leader -- none of these male rulers have done any good lately, so why not a woman take over!!??!!

TENTACLES MAXIMUS, Praetor Primus
- Julius's Younger Brother and Paramour of Empress Chianti

MAXIMUS, brother to the Emperor and an ambitious Senator, is quite vocal about his distaste concerning his brother's recent erratic and strange behavior...mainly because Jack-of-all-Trades, the Emperor's racing stallion took Tentacles's place at the dinner table. Imagine! Usurped by a flea-bitten nag!! Tentacles has secretly vowed to get even with his brother if it's the last thing he does...and to get the ball rolling he has begun an affair with the Empress Chianti and has started to spread dissent and rebellion among the other Senators. If all goes to plan, then there will be a new ruler by the end of this Holiday Festival -- even if someone has to die in order for that to happen!

SCAPULA ERECTUS, Roman Centurion
- A career military man with sights of the Highest Office in Rome - The Dictatorship!

Scapula is a battle-hardened soldier who has seen his share of war and conflict both throughout the Empire. Though not one to shrink from the act of shedding blood, Scapula is tired of the constant military campaigning and longs to settle down in Rome, where he can then pursue his wooing of the Emperor's Greek concubine, Hermaphrodite. His many months away from the city of Rome have made it hard for him to keep hope alive that the lovely Hermaphrodite is truly his...after all, she does spend a lot of time with the Emperor, and if rumors are true, then she will become the next Emperor's concubine as well! Only one way to make sure that he can win her forever...by taking over Rome itself!

HERMAPHRODITE
- the Emperor's Concubine – a beautiful Grecian Slave Girl and also the Emperor's Personal Manicurist and Soothsayer

Hermaphrodite, or just plain 'Dite {pronounced "dighty"} has been living in the Emperor's palace since she was a little girl, the daughter of the Emperor's previous concubine. It is even rumored that she is the Emperor's daughter...which is kind of scary considering that she bathes him on a regular basis -- makes you shudder, doesn't it? A bright, intelligent girl with hopes of a future away from Rome and the back-stabbing intrigue and poisonous atmosphere of the Emperor's palace, she longs to open her own Temp Agency on the outskirts of the Empire, finding jobs for former slaves, exotic dancing girls, and ex-gladiators.

CARRYONUS, of the Samonsonites

- Barbarian -Tribal Prince captured by Scapula Erectus in the Wars of Southern Mauritania

A young prince of a barbarian tribe, Carryonus was captured by Scapula's troops several years ago after a bloody skirmish in the desert lands of Mauritania -- a small country that is a neighbor of Mesopotamia (kinda like Rhode Island is a neighbor of Connecticut) -- this shaggy desert warrior has been scheduled to serve in the Gladiatorial Contests in Honor of the Festival of the Cranky Virgin. Lately, he has been serving in the Emperor's palace, as a stable boy and chief attendant to the Emperor's prize steed, Jack-of-all-Trades. He would like nothing better than to escape the shackles of slavery and escape back to wild hills and dales of his homeland. Oh, yeah...and take a bath too.

FUN FACTS

THE EMPRESS CHIANTI (kë än´te) –
Chianti is the daughter from a long line of Roman nobles and strives to maintain decorum and appearance in all situations. Once, when the Emperor threw-up in public, she laughed and commented, "Oh, look! The Emperor has just taken up performance art!"

TENTACLES MAXIMUS (ten´te- kle´z • maks´ i muz´) –
A living legend in the Roman Senate, Tentacles has been known to stand and filibuster for days on end. Which is surprising, considering there are rumors circulating around the city that his stamina is somewhat lacking in other areas...most notably in the Red Light district.

SCAPULA ERECTUS (skap´ ye le • ĕ rekt´ es) –
The Wars in Mauritania left the noble Scapula haggard and drained...not because of the horrors of war, but mainly because he suffered from heat-stroke and a blistering case of athlete's foot. This condition continues to plague him to this very day.

HERMAPHRODITE (her maf´ro dit´ e) –
Even though she may a mere serving girl in the royal palace Hermaphrodite, (or just plain 'Dite as she prefers to be called, as opposed to Hermaph), has already begun an underground campaign to bring equal rights to all the slaves of Rome. She secretly publishes the radical newspaper, *Serve This*.

CARRYONUS, of the Samonsonites (kar´e ôn es) – While not yet accustomed to working in the palace, Carryonus has developed a real sense of Roman life and in particular, a real 'Roman' attitude. Thus, he has taken to wearing his gladiatorial armor with pride, even when sweeping out the Emperor's stables...in fact he wears it no matter what activity he is doing!

PRODUCTION NOTES

The following notes are given for each cast to consider using so that they may best convey the look and feel that the production aims to achieve. Naturally each cast will have their own ideas and concepts about how best to present the atmosphere and ambience of an ancient Roman abode – but the more Hollywood-esque the better.

COSTUMES – Costumes should be as complete as possible and should give the audience information and clues about each of the characters. For inspiration please take a look at the costumes worn by the actor's in films such as ***Gladiato****r* or ***History of the World, Part I***.

- CARRYONUS – should be dressed as a 'Roman-ized' Barbarian – not in fur and skins, but tunic and sandals.

- MAXIMUS – should be dressed as a Roman Senator.

- CHIANTI – should be dressed as a member of the Roman Elite, see Madeline Kahn in History of the World for inspiration.

- HERMAPHRODITE – should be dressed as an empress's handmaiden – long flowing silks, etc.

- SCAPULA – should be dressed as a Roman Legionnaire.

- **CINNCINATUS** – should be dressed as an Emperor, complete with laurel wreath headband and sandals.

PLAYING SPACE – In addition to the regular set up materials (*fun facts, pencils and WhoDunnit Cards*) the acting area should have three spots on different walls or support beams where items representing Ancient Rome can be placed – ferns, fake marble statues, etc. – all depending on the company budget, of course. Anything you can do to give the playing space the more atmosphere the better you can use it to your advantage and to draw the audience into playing along.

ACT ONE

{*The top of the show should begin with some rousing 'Roman-esque' music, something from the Golden Age of epic Hollywood films like **BEN HUR**, **SPARTACUS**, or possibly, Copeland's **FANFARE FOR THE COMMON MAN**. Then we are treated to a brief Voice Over that sets the stage and mood :*}

***SFX* cue**

VOICE OVER

(*on tape, or microphone; appropriate music in the background*)

256 B. C. E.

Rome - the greatest city in the Western World.
For nearly five hundred years, the magnificent city of Rome has dominated the known world with its Military prowess; educated the world with its learned Philosophy and provided the world with the laws of its Statesmen… and also, shown the world of fashion the amazing versatility of a plain, ordinary sheet.

This then is Rome…

(*singing*)

Rome… Rome, on the Range!!
Where the Ibex and the Antelope play!
Where seldom is heard, a discouraging word
and the skies are not cloudy all day!

{*There is a sudden burst of music: a flourish of trumpets usually associated with the entrance of royalty. Enter into the playing space, a helmeted gladiator, who appears dressed for battle and ready to leap into the Arena…except, instead of a sword and shield, he is wielding a brush and dust-pan.
This is CARRYONUS, barbarian slave, gladiator and stable-boy. With a practiced assurance he sets to his task of dusting the Palace. As he moves about the room he whistles to himself, a tune*

recognizable as the theme to **THE BRIDGE ON THE RIVER KWAI**.
Enter EMPRESS CHIANTI holding a clump of grapes and popping them into her mouth, followed by HERMAPHRODITE who is carrying a bundle of cloth and a vase of flowers}

CHIANTI
(*walking briskly over to the Emperor's 'dais' area – a chair designated as the Emperor's throne*)
Has everything been arranged for the festivities and orgy tonight, my dear 'Dite?
You did make special arrangements for the Emperor, yes? Due to his special back ailment?

HERMAPHRODITE
Yes, your majesty.

CHIANTI
(*sighing heavily, a little exasperated*)
Please, 'Dite, don't call me 'your majesty'...
I prefer the term Highness...it sounds so much more...lofty.

CARRYONUS
(*who snapped to attention at their entrance...suddenly leaps forward before the Empress and delivers his traditional salute, bellowing it out*)
WE, WHO ARE ABOUT TO DIE, SALUTE YOU!!!

CHIANTI & HERMAPHRODITE
(*both together*)
AHHHHHHHH!!

HERMAPHRODITE
What the heck are you doing!

CHIANTI
Moronic savage! You nearly gave me a heart attack!

CARRYONUS
(*dropping to one knee and bowing his head*)
A thousand pardons, my queen.
I was only giving the Gladiator's Traditional Salute!
I meant no harm to you...your slave girl...or the blood pump that beats so proudly in your more than ample bosomy, busty chest.

CHIANTI
(*a little taken a-back*)
My what!?!? Beating in my where!?!?

MAXIMUS
(*who comes trotting in, tightening his belt or 'zipping up' his toga*)
What's going on in here? I heard the screams all the way down in the bathitorium...
Is anything the matter?

HERMAPHRODITE
This hairy primate nearly scared her Highness to death with his battle cry.

CHIANTI
Maximus!!...You must do something about that...creature!
I don't know whatever possessed Julius to take him into our home.

MAXIMUS
Wasn't he a "gift" from that braggart, Scapula? A prize taken in some obscure battle?

CHIANTI
Oh, yes...now I remember...he brought this person back to serve as Julius's stable-boy.
What are you doing in here, heathen...don't you have some dung to be dunging, or something?

HERMAPHRODITE
I think the Emperor requested that he patrol the palace grounds...the Emperor has been a little paranoid lately.

CARRYONUS
(*still on one knee, but removing his helmet*)
What your serving wench relates is true, my queen...

HERMAPHRODITE
(*taking offense*)
I am not a serving wench...I'm a concubine!

CARRYONUS
(*ignoring her*)
The Emperor did request that I secure the palace grounds for his safety.
He feels that his life is in danger.

MAXIMUS
The Emperor's life in danger? That is absurd!
Who in all of Rome would be so bold as to threaten the life of our beloved Emperor?!

CHIANTI
(*elbowing him, and speaking out of the side of her mouth*)

Give it a rest, Max.
He may be your brother, but you detest him as much as the next man.

HERMAPHRODITE
(*aside*)
Or woman for that matter...

CHIANTI
What was that, 'Dite?
Did you say something?

HERMAPHRODITE
(*smiling sheepishly and struggling to cover*)
Uh...I said...O roman doors that clatter...
A Greek saying...that means...Roman doors are...noisy...

{*CHIANTI eyes her suspiciously and then turns back to MAXIMUS*}

CHIANTI
Are we sure we need extra security?
Won't there be a retinue of guard's from Scapula's troops here tonight because of the Festival?

MAXIMUS
(*turning back to CARRYONUS*)
Yes, the Empress is right...
Tell us why these extra security measures are necessary, young barbarian...

CARRYONUS
(*still on one knee*)
Most noble and gracious Senator Testicles...

MAXIMUS
Ahem! The name is Tentacles, dear boy... But, did you hear? Finally a servant who knows how to show respect!

CHIANTI
Yes! And did you hear how he referred to me? "My Queen...!" I don't think I've ever been addressed so formally before!

MAXIMUS
Not so, my dear! Remember that ragged prisoner from Troy? Just before he was killed by the lions in the Coliseum, he referred to you as the Queen of All Mothers, remember?

CHIANTI
Yes, but this young brute seems so much more sincere! Perhaps he is not so savage after all!

HERMAPHRODITE
(*half to herself, disgusted at this display*)
Ugh! What a bunch of losers!

CHIANTI
'DITE!
If you're going to say something I wish you would speak up, and share it with the rest of us!

HERMAPHRODITE
(*smiling facetiously*)
Uh...no... That's okay!

{*CHIANTI eyes her suspiciously once again and then turns back to CARRYONUS and MAXIMUS*}

CHIANTI
Please...continue with your explanation, noble barbarian...

CARRYONUS
Very well, my Queen.
(*pause for CHIANTI as she smirks in HERMAPHRODITE's direction*)
As you said...I was captured by the patrician, Scapula Erectus, in the Wars against my homeland of Mauritania...

MAXIMUS
Oh, yes...I remember now...
That buffoon Scapula had led his troops into an ambush and this brute here saved them...
As a reward, Scapula enslaved him and brought him back here to serve in the Gladiator school!

CARRYONUS
(*continuing to clean as though he were reliving the event, using his brush as a sword*)
'Tis true, most honorable Senator Testicles!

MAXIMUS
Tentacles! The name is Tentacles...

CARRYONUS
(*ignoring him and continuing with his fervent speech*)
The battle that day was fierce and heated, men fell screaming to the left and to the right!
And many horses and pack animals were slain as well...for this was in the time before the ASPCA...

HERMAPHRODITE
(*to an audience member, and starting to sit down*)
Scoot over will ya?
I can see this is gonna be one of those long-winded explanations...

CARRYONUS
(*leaping over next to her and with a great display of faux parrying and thrusting*)
Not so, serving wench!

HERMAPHRODITE
(*really miffed now, she quickly grasps his ear and twists it violently*)
Look, bub...I prefer the term serving girl...all right!!
Call me a serving wench one more time and I'll rip off your preator and shove it up your Aegean! Got me!?!?!?

CARRYONUS
(*in obvious pain*)
Ow! Yes...yes...!! Leggo!! Leggo!! You're ripping my ear off!!

CHIANTI
All right! Enough!!! 'Dite! Release him at once!
(*after HERMAPHRODITE lets him go*)
So...You rescued the General Scapula and he enslaved you, is that correct?

CARRYONUS
(*still smarting from HERMAPHRODITE's ear-wrenching*)
Yes, my queen, but I was slave by my own will. For I soon came to see the wisdom of General Scapula's plan. Since the time of my capture my homeland has been at peace with the might of the Roman Empire... And according to the treaty signed between us,

no blood has been spilt between our peoples since I, the Prince of Loins, now serve as the Emperor's bodyguard!

CHIANTI
Prince of Loins? Don't you mean Prince of Lions?

CARRYONUS
(*dropping character for a brief second*)
Uh, yeah...must've been a spelling error in the script.
(*back in character and quite proud of both the following facts*)
Yes! I am a prince of noble birth in my homeland...though here in Rome I am lower than dirt!

CHIANTI
Well...!!!
It certainly is quite a change of pace to meet a servant who appreciates his station in life!
(*she glares evilly at HERMAPHRODITE*)
But, tell us, Prince of Loins...ahem, Lions...what is your name?

HERMAPHRODITE
(*aside*)
This guy's been living on the palace grounds for nearly five years...and she just now wants to know his name?

MAXIMUS
Please! There are nearly 250 servants working here in the palace...you can't expect us to memorize all of their names...that would be too hard!!

HERMAPHRODITE
(*aside*)
From what I've heard...nothing is hard for him anymore!

CHIANTI
'DITE!!! Please!!!
One more outburst from you and I will see to it that you are barred from the orgy tonight!
(*to CARRYONUS*)
Now, you were saying...?

CARRYONUS
My name is Carryonus of the Samsonites.

CHIANTI
Samsonites?

SCAPULA
(*who has entered on CHIANTI's last line*)
Yes, Samsonites... a small tribe of bronze-age savages living in the deserts of Mauritania...
Not very good fighters, but they do make excellent luggage...

CHIANTI
(*spinning around, surprised*)
General Scapula!

HERMAPHRODITE
I gotta get outta here! (*aside, to audience member*) Quick! Hide me!

MAXIMUS
(*equally surprised and obviously feigning friendship*)
Scapula, my dear friend...how are you, you great fool!
(*quickly moving to wipe something off of SCAPULA's armor*)
...uh, I mean...is that drool?

SCAPULA
(*also examining his armor*)
No...not drool...I would've remembered drooling...

CHIANTI
What an unexpected surprise!
We didn't expect to see you until the Festival tonight!

SCAPULA
(*still wiping his breast-plate*)
Well, I just thought I would drop in a tad early to check up on my prize pupil...

{*He steps closer to CARRYONUS, and they exchange a high-five*}

SCAPULA (*both together*)	**CARRYONUS** (*both together*)
What it is!	What's up, my man!?

MAXIMUS
(*a little snidely*)
An interesting display of machismo... But tell me, is that a traditional warrior's salute?

CARRYONUS
Verily, Senator Testicles...

MAXIMUS
(*getting red in the face*)
Tentacles! The name is Tentacles...

CARRYONUS
'Tis a salute of respect and honor 'tween two fearless heroes who have faced each other on the bloody field of battle.

SCAPULA
Yes, yes...no need to get upset, friend Maximus... If you wish, the Prince and I can show you other variations of the warrior's salute...most notably the Two-Fisted Chest Punch, the Neck and Shoulder Grab-and-Shake, or the equally famous Behind-the-Back Gluteus Slap.

CHIANTI
(*very, very excited*)
Ooooh!!! The last one...Show us the last one!!!

HERMAPHRODITE
Easy!! Take it easy...try not to look so eager, your highness!!
(*aside, to audience member*)
Have you ever seen anyone so desperate?!

MAXIMUS
(*stepping quickly over to CHIANTI*)
Ah, the serving girl, does have a point, my dear... What would your husband say if he were to see you drooling over the ritual greeting practices of the military class?

CHIANTI
(*still very, very excited*)
My husband? Emperor Oldas Dirtus? Probably nothing! The man can't hear much less do anything!
(*to SCAPULA*)
So tell me General, will any of this Gluteus slapping be taking place at the Festival tonight?

SCAPULA
I'm afraid not, my queen.
I will be the only member of the Roman Legions present at tonight's festivities.
All the other centurions are off to the Coliseum to attend that silly Elton Janus concert...
He has that hit song you know, "Goodbye Roman Brick Road".

CHIANTI
(*suddenly very, very upset*)
What!?!

MAXIMUS
Yes...I heard that.
And I was coming to tell you that the Senators maybe a bit late tonight, if they are coming at all. It appears the Emperor has called an emergency session to determine whether or not some stupid proposal is fit to be passed into law… someone suggested that horse of his, Jack-of-all-Trades should be made a Senator.

CHIANTI
But...but this cannot be!
I have spent countless hours over the last several weeks...working so hard to make sure that everything for the Festival was going to be so perfect!
How can it be perfect, if I am the only one attending!?

CARRYONUS
But you will not be the only one attending, my queen...
Myself and twenty other gladiators will be posted as guard, the greased and oiled Trojan all-male acrobatic team is scheduled to

perform, and there will be thirty blemish-free, tanned and toned Greek eunuchs serving as wine bearer's and towel boys.

CHIANTI
(*suddenly cheered again*)
Oh...yes! That's right!
I almost forgot about the towel boys!

HERMAPHRODITE
(*aside, to audience member*)
Right...!!! Like she's gonna miss the chance at a rub down!

SCAPULA
Tell me, dear Empress...Will the Emperor be making an appearance before the Festival...there is a matter of some importance I wish to discuss with him.

CHIANTI
(*with a sniff of displeasure*)
Actually, I believe that the little old windbag is supposed to stop by here any moment now to give his stamp of approval to the floral arrangements that 'Dite has picked out for tonight's revelry.

CARRYONUS
Then I must return quickly to my security detail...
Forgive me, most noble Empress and most esteemed Senator, but I will refrain from further gladiatorial salutes since they are an offense to your delicate natures...

MAXIMUS
Nonsense, dear boy, since we now know them to be nothing but courtesy...
Please...feel free to salute us anytime!

{*CARRYONUS then moves center stage and addresses the entire ensemble*}

CARRYONUS

Then I salute you in the tradition and language of my people!
(*he slaps his left hand on his right shoulder*)
SUS!!
(*slaps his right hand on his left shoulder*)
SUS!!
(*finally slapping both hands on his rear-end and thrusting his pelvis forward*)
GATUNE KOYARIM!!!
[*pronounced: gah-tooney koy-ar-rim*]

{*CARRYONUS then turns crispy and marches from the room. The others stare after him for a beat, CHIANTI, MAXIMUS, and SCAPULA, all wearing expressions of confusion...not wanting to admit that they don't understand what just happened. HERMAPHRODITE, on the other hand, is trying very hard not to laugh out loud, knowing full well that they were just terribly insulted*}

MAXIMUS

Fascinating, isn't it?
The way other cultures show their respect...

SCAPULA

(*trying really hard to cover for his ignorance*)
Yes...yes it is, my friend. I believe this particular Mauritanian salute derives from an ancient greeting to their primitive gods... Having spent a number of years here in the palace, he has obviously come to view you, Empress, and the Emperor as extensions of his people's own deities!!

CHIANTI
(*smiling through her confusion*)
Well...That was certainly...interesting. I've never been saluted that way before.

HERMAPHRODITE
(*aside, giggling to audience member*)
At least not in public!

CHIANTI
'DITE!!!
Why are you laughing? Are you aware of something we are not?

HERMAPHRODITE
(*struggling not to laugh aloud*)
No, no...your highness!
I was just...thinking of something...a joke, one of the other serving girls told me...

SCAPULA
(*sauntering over to HERMAPHRODITE*)
Well...don't hold back, my little Grecian urn...
(*he starts to stroke her hair*)
What is it? Tell us your little joke...

HERMAPHRODITE
(*miffed that he has gotten this close to her*)
All right...you asked for it...
What's the difference between a Greek from Athens and a Greek from Thebes?

{*The other three think for a moment then smile and shake their heads*}

SCAPULA
I don't know...What is the difference between a Greek from Athens and a Greek from Thebes?

HERMAPHRODITE
(*takes him by the shoulders and then bringing her knee into his crotch as she says the punchline*)
Nuttin'!!!!

{*SCAPULA crumples to the ground with a squeak, and the other two make sour faces and suck the air through their teeth-- as if to say, "Oooh...that's gotta hurt!"*}

MAXIMUS
(*already beginning to head for the exit*)
Well...not the best joke I've ever heard...but it certainly has a kick at the end doesn't it?

CHIANTI
Yes! Quite a wallop I must say!

MAXIMUS
Chianti, my dear, may I talk to you in private please, out here in the hall?
I have a message you may be interested in hearing

CHIANTI
Yes! Certainly!
The air in here has gotten a little swollen...ah, stiff...uh...Stuffy! Right this way, Maximus!

{*They both exit quickly, trying their best to avoid HERMAPHRODITE on the way out. HERMAPHRODITE stands with her arms crossed watching them exit, then walks over to where SCAPULA is laying*}

HERMAPHRODITE
Oh, get up.
I didn't kick you that hard.

SCAPULA
(*struggling to his feet, his voice still high-pitched*)
Hard enough!

HERMAPHRODITE
What are you doing here anyway? I thought we agreed that you weren't going to show up here until after the Senate meeting...you know, the one where you were supposed to...

SCAPULA
(*clapping his hand across her mouth, his voice finally returning to normal*)
SSsssssshhhhh!!
The palace walls have ears! It is not safe to talk of our secret plot here!

HERMAPHRODITE
(*pulling his hand down and pushing him away*)
Oh, please!!!
Everyone in the palace has a secret plot!
If you're not running around arranging a secret plot you're considered socially inept.

SCAPULA
Yes...well...I still do not think it is prudent to discuss our plan here in the Emperor's audience chamber.

HERMAPHRODITE
What's the matter, Scap'?
You afraid of some sort of divine retribution or something...like the Furies chasing Orestes?

SCAPULA
Exactly! I don't want to get (*pronouncing it: or-rested*) arrested!

HERMAPHRODITE
That's arrested, bonehead!
And don't worry about it...if you get caught they're not gonna arrest you...

SCAPULA
Well...! That's a relief!

HERMAPHRODITE
(*moving over to where she left the flowers*)
Nah...if you get caught, most likely they'll kill you right then and there.

SCAPULA
(*shocked*)
They wouldn't dare! I am a great Roman general!
Besides, my intentions are strictly of the highest order...what I do; I do for the good of Rome!!

HERMAPHRODITE
(*arranging the flowers just so, and spraying them with a perfume spritzer*)
You don't really think anybody's gonna buy that line of bull, do you, Scap'...?
You're doing this 'cause you're hoping to get something from me...
(*shaking her head, and half to herself*)
How on earth did I get mixed up with you in the first place?
I must've been drinking something really strange that night...!!

SCAPULA
(*hefting a clay bottle up for her to see, and then pouring some into a goblet*)
A little of this Etruscan elderberry wine, I believe...
(*he saunters over to her, offering the her the cup*)
And it's true! I do this for the good of Rome...and a little nookie from my Grecian Cookie!

HERMAPHRODITE
(*spinning quickly to face him*)
Uh-uh-ah! The job ain't done yet, remember, General?
No peeking into the cookie jar until the Emperor is dead and gone!

SCAPULA
(*setting the cup aside*)
Ah...it is as good as done, 'Dite!
So...why not give me a little nibble...just to tide me over, eh?

HERMAPHRODITE
(*smiling wickedly*)
You don't want another swift kick to the Roman Fountain, do you?

SCAPULA
(*stopping dead in his tracks, and slowly covering himself*)
Uh...on second thought...perhaps I should go see if the Emperor has arrived at the Senate.
I wouldn't want to miss his big speech on the virtues of horse-play in politics...

HERMAPHRODITE
You do that...and don't forget... No dead Emperor...no Grecian holiday!

SCAPULA
(*blowing her a kiss*)
Until the deed is done...Farewell, my sweet!

{*Exit SCAPULA*}

HERMAPHRODITE
(*sniffing the clay bottle of wine*)
Remind me to tell him how to pick his wines...smells like it's been strained through his breeches!

{*Enter CARRYONUS, bearing an arm-load of pillows. He sets them down and sneaks up behind HERMAPHRODITE*}

CARRYONUS
(*loudly*)
GREETINGS, SERVING GIRL OF OUR MOST NOBLE QUEEN!

HERMAPHRODITE
(*as before, startled out of her wits*)
AHHHH!!!

(*after calming herself*)
Do you have to keep doing that!?! (*she eyes him up and down a moment*) Oh, by the way, Thundar...you can drop the 'faithful servant' act...okay?
You ain't as loyal as everybody thinks you are...

CARRYONUS
(*a look of shock on his face*)
What means this?
I am the most trustworthy and humble of the Emperor's guard!

HERMAPHRODITE
(*with a smirk*)
Yeah, right...and I'm the Queen of Sheba!
Listen, bucko...You ain't the only one around here who speaks Mauritanian...'kay?
That weren't no 'warrior's salute' you gave to the Empress and Senator Minuteness.

CARRYONUS
(*placing the pillows in seat-like arrangements around the room*)
Well, perhaps you speak a different dialect of Mauritanian than I...that was indeed a warrior's salute!

HERMAPHRODITE
Uh-huh. And I suppose telling other warrior's that they bathe in sheep droppings is a sign of real respect in Mauritania.

CARRYONUS
(*caught, struggling to cover...but still trying to act casual*)
Indeed!
We take baths in ram's droppings...so that...
We can...announce to our enemies...

That we are unafraid of their clean smelling armies!
If a soldier smells bad, then he fights more ferociously!

HERMAPHRODITE

(*raising her eyebrows in disbelief*)
I don't even wanna know if that is true or not...
So let's just agree to disagree on the meaning of your salute, 'kay?
Besides...I don't think you're as 'dumb and savage' as you make out to be...
What are you hiding, Carryonus? Are you harboring a secret plot to overthrow the Roman Government?

CARRYONUS

(*he stamps his foot on the ground several times and does his best Mr. Ed*)
Nay...I tell you...Nay!!

HERMAPHRODITE

Take it easy there, National Velvet...I just meant...are you one of us?
I mean, everybody around here is looking to take down the Emperor, right?
I just figured you being captured when the Roman army conquered your homeland...

CARRYONUS

Nonsense! Why would I want to destroy the one man who is responsible for the elevation of my tribe from the barbaric ways of our past? Without the good works of my Emperor, my people would still be languishing in the dark and uncivilized savage practices of our ancestors...
Brutal war...bloody, heathen sacrifices, and the blasphemous worship of idols!

HERMAPHRODITE
Right...instead of the civilized Roman way of life...which just so happens to practice -- brutal war, bloody, gladiatorial sacrifices, and the worship of idols...

CARRYONUS
(*a little flustered now*)
What are you getting at, serving girl?
Can you not see that I have work to do?

HERMAPHRODITE
Look...you are no better off now, than when that bonehead Scapula dragged you here in chains...Just because you're not wearing them anymore, don't necessarily mean that they're not there!
You were brought to Rome a slave, and that's what you'll be...until the day you die...or until the Emperor sets you free...which isn't gonna happen! Believe me, I know!

CARRYONUS
(*his eyes narrowing*)
So...what you are saying is...that unless something happens to Emperor Cincinnatus...

HERMAPHRODITE
You're stuck arranging pillows and shoveling horse dung for the rest of your life!

CARRYONUS
(*his back to her, he places a large dagger or something similar behind one of the pillows*)
Hmmmm. You have given me food for thought, serving girl.
I shall consider what you have said...

HERMAPHRODITE
(*making her way to the exit*)
Don't just consider it, luggage-boy...if you don't do something to improve your situation -- who the heck is going to?

{*Exit HERMAPHRODITE*}

CARRYONUS
(*aside, taking the audience into his confidence*)
For a Greek, she's a real pain in the Assyrian, isn't she? It is a good thing that my father said, "Son, never to listen to the advice of women..."
(*picking up the goblet of wine and setting it back on the table*)
Of course that could also explain why he had seventeen ex-wives... Perhaps I shall seek out this serving girl later, to hear more of this 'plot' business...

{*Re-enter MAXIMUS and CHIANTI, still whispering lowly*}

CHIANTI
But are you sure the Emperor specifically asked that the Senate consider Jack-of-all-Trade's measure today?

MAXIMUS
Correct, my Empress...all slaves taken before the Festival of the Horny Toad, that being five years ago this coming week, are to be given full rights as Roman citizens!

CHIANTI
(*noticing CARRYONUS*)
Uh, Maximus, darling...perhaps we should discuss this later...when we are alone...

MAXIMUS
(*not seeing CARRYONUS and not heeding CHIANTI*)
But we must discuss it! If former slaves were to become Roman citizens...then they would receive the right to ascend to the position of Senator! It's bad enough that the old goat got his horse a seat in the Forum...but to allow a former slave...!

CARRYONUS
(*who has walked up behind MAXIMUS, clears his throat*)
GREETINGS, ILLUSTRIOUS BROTHER OF OUR MOST NOBLE EMPEROR!

MAXIMUS
(*startled*)
AAAHHH!! What the heck are you doing here!?!
I mean...how fare you, gallant Samsonite...?

CARRYONUS
Good evening once again, dear Empress...and honorable Senator Testicles.

MAXIMUS
(*getting red in the face*)
Tentacles! The name is Tentacles...

CARRYONUS
Yes, of course...I was just arranging a few, last minute details for the Emperor's arrival.
I go now to stand by the front portal to await the Emperor.

MAXIMUS
Good...you do that. Sneak up on our glorious leader for a change!

CHIANTI
Never mind him, Carryonus...He's just a little upset right now. Please...take your post. And be sure to sound the trumpet upon the Emperor's arrival.

{*CARRYONUS starts to make his exit, then at the door turns and salutes them once more*}

CARRYONUS
(*giving the same physical salute as before, but delivering this line at the end*)
May all the fleas of the desert infest the armpits of your enemies!!

{*Exit CARRYONUS*}

MAXIMUS
(*looking after him with suspicion*)
I can never be sure if he is honestly paying tribute, or just making fun of us...

CHIANTI
Oh...What does it matter?
We have more important things to discuss...what about the 'plan'?

MAXIMUS
Not to worry my sweet, everything is going according to schedule...in fact the Emperor should be arriving at the Senate any moment now, and when he does...KA-POW!!

CHIANTI

Ka-pow? What are you going to do...shoot him out of a catapult?

MAXIMUS

No...I just meant that...oh, nevermind!
The important thing is, I got all the other Senators worked up into such a fury over the old geezer's latest horse-drawn proposal, that they all arrived this morning carrying their favorite weapons! Knives, short swords, spears...even old Flavius wheeled in a huge pot of boiling oil!

CHIANTI

You mean that...?

MAXIMUS

That's right! Once the Emperor makes his way into the Forum...KA-POW!!

CHIANTI

Brilliant! And then you and I can get down to business!

MAXIMUS

That's right! With all the legislators after him...
There's no way anyone can suspect us of complicity in his death!

CHIANTI

Wait!
Will the people feel that the Emperor's death is necessary?
You know he's always had a way of getting them on his side!
If they rise up against whoever kills him...

MAXIMUS

Why do you think I'm here and not at the Forum!?! There's no way I'm gonna be around when that angry mob starts looking for someone to pin this on!
If there's one thing I know how to do, it's how to be in the right place at the wrong time!

CHIANTI
(*a little confused*)
Isn't that supposed to be the other way around?
Oh...who cares! And once the mob finds someone to blame, we can sweep in as the voices of reason, calm everybody down, and get down to the business of festival, party and orgy planning!

MAXIMUS
And running the Empire...

CHIANTI
Oh, yes, yes ...that as well! But parties are so much more fun! And I know exactly how I want my first New Empire party to start
--
With decadence, debauchery and dancing!
Maximus, my darling! I cannot wait until the Emperor is dead!

MAXIMUS
Neither can I...it has been so long since I was made to feel like a real woman!

CHIANTI
Wait...shouldn't that be the other way around?
Oh, nevermind! Oh, Maximus!
(*after a brief kiss*)
Or should I say...Oh, Testicles!!

{*just then, the sound of the royal trumpets is heard, announcing the imminent arrival of the Emperor*}

MAXIMUS

(*spinning towards the entrance*)
I...I don't understand!
How can the Emperor be here? I thought for sure the senators would have axed him at the Forum!

CHIANTI

(*also reacting to the sound of the horns*)
Oh, no! Now what shall we do?

{*enter into the playing space, the EMPEROR, who shambles along in an elderly dash. He sports about eight or nine daggers sticking out of his back, and he shuffle-runs about the room in slo-mo*}

EMPEROR JULIUS

Help! Assassins! Killers!

MAXIMUS

(*stepping back to allow the "speeding" EMPEROR by*)
I don't understand!
How can he survive with all those knives sticking out of his back!?

EMPEROR JULIUS

Killers! Assassins! Help!

CHIANTI

(*to MAXIMUS, and also side-stepping to let the 'running' EMPEROR by*)

It's simple really...when he was born; it was divined by the sacred Oracle that Julius was to live a long and successful life...but that death would take him by an unseen hand...
Naturally Julius took this to mean from behind...

{*Enter into the room, both HERMAPHRODITE and CARRYONUS, gazing in awe at the pin-cushioned EMPEROR*}

EMPEROR JULIUS
(*re-acting to the newcomers with still more shuffling about the room*)
Assassins! Bad men with big knives!

CHIANTI
(*finishing her explanation to MAXIMUS*)
So his surgeon recommended that leeches be attached to his back, and those little bloodsuckers were left on his flesh a tad too long...they just slurped the nerve endings right out from under his skin.
He hasn't been able to feel anything anywhere for most of his life.

HERMAPHRODITE
Oh! How awful!

CARRYONUS
A most disturbing case of sensory deprivation!

{*all of the others, including the EMPEROR, turn to gaze at CARRYONUS in wonder at his use of this expression*}

CARRYONUS
What? I'm a savage...but I'm an educated savage, okay!?

EMPEROR JULIUS
(*still shuffling around the room, until he gets near the goblet, from which he takes a gulp*)
Killers! Stabbing! (*takes a drink*) Gotta run...hide me!

CHIANTI
(*a little irritated with this now*)
Oh, calm down Julius! You can't feel anything remember?
Just try to think of this as one of those painful times we tried to consummate our marriage...
A lot of rushing, a lot of screaming, and no sensation!

HERMAPHRODITE
(*feeling sorry for CHIANTI*)
Wow...I guess you got a pretty good reason for being so bitchy all the time then, huh?

CHIANTI
You got no idea, sister!!

MAXIMUS
All right, everyone calm down!
We have to help our Emperor!

EMPEROR JULIUS
Uh-oh! I gotta bad feeling about this!
(*with a sudden gasp and gurgle, the EMPEROR begins to sink slowly to the floor*)
Looks like...I'm a' dyin'!!!

{*The EMPEROR then goes through a semi-protracted death scene -- just don't let it go on too long!!!*}

CARRYONUS
Boy...I'm glad that's finally over!

MAXIMUS
Tell me about it... If it had gone on any longer, we'd have to start payin' the wait staff Over Time!

CHIANTI
(*elated*)
He's dead! The Emperor is dead!
(*and then feigning sadness*)
Uh...I mean...oh, Julius...Julius! Whatever shall Rome do now?!

HERMAPHRODITE
Someone has assassinated the Emperor!

MAXIMUS
We must inform the citizens of Rome!

CARRYONUS
Wait! I don't think that's such a good idea!
I mean...Won't that cause wide spread panic and confusion? Don't you think we should try to solve this mystery ourselves...for the sake of Rome?!

CHIANTI
The noble savage is right! Only we can figure out what was the real cause of Julius' death!
It was obviously not caused by those daggers and knives sticking out of his back

HERMAPHRODITE
But the party...!? It's supposed to start any minute now!

MAXIMUS
All right... here's what we do...
You girls distract the party guests and usher them into the banquet hall...Carryonus and I will take the Emperor's body and secret it in his bed-chamber...then we all meet back here after the desert course and discuss what our options are!

CHIANTI
Good thinking, Maximus...but wait! Where is Scapula!?

CARRYONUS
Well, he and the Emperor are being played by the same actor...

ALL
SSSsssssssshhhhhh!

HERMAPHRODITE
Oh, the General's probably around here somewhere...
Come on...we gotta get moving before those guests arrive!

{*Exit CHIANTI and HERMAPHRODITE*}

MAXIMUS
(*picking up the EMPEROR's legs*)
Well...come along, Samsonite... Let's get the old goat out of here!
**

CARRYONUS
(*motioning to the audience*)

But what about these folks here...what do we do about them?

MAXIMUS
Them!? Who cares about them!
They get to eat ice cream while we get to haul this tub of lard out of here!

CARRYONUS
Hmmm. I guess you're right...I hope you folks appreciate this!
And don't anybody touch anything! It could screw up the crime scene!
We'll be back shortly!

{Exit CARRYONUS and MAXIMUS carrying the body of the EMPEROR}

** *{It is possible that venues will want to run ACTS I and II back to back – if that is the case – use the following alternative scene instead of the exit to the EMPEROR's bed-chamber}*

CHIANTI
Good thinking, Maximus...but wait! Where is Scapula!?

CARRYONUS
Well, he and the Emperor are being played by the same actor...

ALL
SSSsssssssshhhhhh!

HERMAPHRODITE
Oh, the General's probably around here somewhere...
Come on...we gotta get moving before those guests arrive!

MAXIMUS

Samsonite… help me get the body into the bed-chamber…

CARRYONUS

Uh, alright… but no kinky stuff. I ain't that type of body guard.

{Exit CARRYONUS and MAXIMUS carrying the body of the EMPEROR}

CHIANTI

Dite, stay here and make sure everything is cleaned up … I don't want any of the guests to see things in disarray! I am going out to see if anyone has arrived yet!

{Exit CHIANTI}

HERMAPHRODITE

Perfect… just typical how she leaves me to clean up the mess around here!
(*she moves about the space, stopping to bend over near a patron and then jumping up as if pinched*)
Touch me like that again, Senator Flatulus, and I'll see to it that you never get to attend one of the Empresses orgies again! She don't let no one in who ain't got a working faucet...if you catch my drip...uh, drift!!!

{At this point the show can continue as ACT II}

END ACT ONE

ACT TWO

SFX CUE

{*If the show is performed with a break between ACTS I and II – use the following as the opening segment for the opening of ACT II: The second act opens much like the first, with a flare of dramatic Hollywood Epic music, followed by a blaring of trumpets. Then we hear the canned laughter and shouts of a loud raucous party going on outside of the playing area. After a moment or two of this, in stumbles HERMAPHRODITE, her hair askew and trying to adjust her dress. She yells out the doorway to some party guest*}

HERMAPHRODITE

Touch me like that again, Senator Flatulus, and I'll see to it that you never get to attend one of the Empresses orgies again! She don't let no one in who ain't got a working faucet...if you catch my drip...uh, drift!!!

{*She makes her way across the room and begins searching through the pillows that CARRYONUS laid out earlier. During her investigation, CARRYONUS enters and observes her for a moment...When she gets close to the pillows where he hid the dagger, he announces his presence by shouting at the top of his lungs:*}

CARRYONUS
(*shouting*)
HAIL TO THEE, OH SERVING WENCH OF THE EMPEROR!!

HERMAPHRODITE
(*as before, startled out of her wits*)
AHHHH!!!
(*after calming herself*)
Do you have to keep doing that!?!

CARRYONUS
Yes! It is my warrior nature!

HERMAPHRODITE
What the heck are you doing in here anyway?
Aren't you supposed to be guarding the Emperor...or what's left of him?

CARRYONUS
Ah, well...seeing how the Emperor is now nothing more than a pincushion...
I thought I would just pop back in here and continue straightening the pillows, as per my job description.

HERMAPHRODITE
(*not completely convinced of this*)
Uh-huh. You've just come in here to fluff the pillows...
You sure it wasn't to get rid of the evidence?

CARRYONUS
Evidence? I don't know what you mean...

HERMAPHRODITE
(*reaching beneath the pillows and pulling out the dagger CARRYONUS placed there earlier*)

You wanna rephrase that, Thundar...Or are you gonna continue to deny that this little pig-sticker isn't yours? Thought you were pretty slick didn't you? I saw you hide it earlier, when you thought I wasn't looking...

CARRYONUS

(*his pride kicking in*)
All right, I admit it! I hid the knife!
Its blade is covered in the deadly poison of the yellow-spotted fuzzy scorpion; a deadly insect found only in my desert homeland...one drop of its venom is enough to kill ten elephants!

HERMAPHRODITE

So...you hid this poisoned dagger, hoping for a chance to use it on the old geezer?
You took what I told you to heart after all, eh?
You were gonna kill the Emperor in order to free yourself from bondage!

CARRYONUS

Nay! That is completely untrue...
The bondage I rather enjoyed...
No, I had more personal reasons for wanting the Emperor dead.

HERMAPHRODITE

Well, don't keep us in suspense...what are these personal reasons that would cause you to kill Rome's leader?

CARRYONUS

(*glancing around the room, then in a stage whisper*)
I am the ring-leader of the U. S. S. R. -- the United Slaves and Servants Rebellion!

HERMAPHRODITE
(*noticing SCAPULA who is just entering*)
The what? I'm sorry I couldn't hear you...could you repeat that?

CARRYONUS
(*angered, raising his voice to a shout*)
The United Slaves and Servants Rebellion! I am its ring-leader!!

SCAPULA
(*walking in on CARRYONUS's shout*)
Carryonus! I am shocked! And after all that Rome has done for you!

HERMAPHRODITE
Better arrest him, General...looks like we caught our killer!

SCAPULA
Killer? Who's dead?

CARRYONUS
The Emperor, Generally Erect!

SCAPULA
Really!?! Rumor had it that the poor man was impotent...

CARRYONUS
No! It is the Emperor who is dead...you are Erectus, General!

SCAPULA
(*covering himself, then realizing CARRYONUS's mistake*)
That's General Erectus, bonehead! And what do you mean the Emperor is dead!

HERMAPHRODITE
Weren't you here when...?
No! That's right! You weren't here!
Maybe I was jumping to conclusions about you Thundar, maybe you're not the real killer after all...Our good friend, the General here, wasn't with us when we saw the Emperor come running in stuck with all them daggers...

CARRYONUS
You speak the truth, serving girl!
(*grabbing the poisoned dagger and advancing on SCAPULA*)
Tell us General...where were you when the Emperor came running in from the Senate...
Or is that just what you wanted everyone to think?

SCAPULA
(*backing away from the advancing CARRYONUS*)
What are you talking about!?! I did not kill Emperor Cincinnatus! I was in the bathatorium...taking care of some unfinished business...

HERMAPHRODITE
Uh-huh, sure...And I assume you're gonna tell us you've been in there this entire time, huh?
Even through all the commotion that's been going on since the start of the orgy...

SCAPULA
As I said...I was taking care of business, my constitutionals have been known to average three hours or more!...Besides the Emperor had left his copy of Gladiators Illustrated in there...

CARRYONUS
(*less menacing now*)
Ooooohh! Was the swimsuit issue?

SCAPULA
Yes! But I was only reading the articles...

HERMAPHRODITE
Right! That's a pretty weak alibi, General. What do you think the Empress and Senator Minimal are gonna say when you hand them that line of bull?

SCAPULA
Well, perhaps I will tell them that it was all part of a certain plan...a plot if you will...cooked up by the Emperor's own concubine...a certain Grecian slave girl who had harbored a deep and unmitigated hatred for the Roman Empire since being sold into captivity several years ago!

CARRYONUS
Really? I'd sooner believe the Gladiator's Illustrated line...

HERMAPHRODITE
(*walking up to SCAPULA and with an evil smirk*)
Guess that little tale of yours isn't gonna hold up... (*glancing down at his mid-section*)
But then again that's par for the course for you, right General?

SCAPULA
Why...you evil little witch!
I should have known better than to let myself get involved with you!

HERMAPHRODITE
Involved!? Please...one brief, and I do mean brief, tumble in the sauna does not mean we're involved.

CARRYONUS
Wait a minute...Earlier this evening, the Greek girl tried to persuade me that I should assassinate the Emperor in order to free myself from my own shackles of bondage!

SCAPULA
Carryonus! I had no idea you were into that sort of thing!

CARRYONUS
(*glaring at him*)
Are you really this dumb, or are you just playing?

SCAPULA
(*haughtily*)
I never play, Carryonus...and when I do play, I play to win!

CARRYONUS & HERMAPHRODITE
(*glancing at each other, then together*)
He really is that dumb.

CARRYONUS
What I was trying to say, is that maybe what General Moronicus accuses you of...isn't so farfetched after all, 'Dite! If you were bold enough to try to entice me into killing the Emperor, then who knows how many others you've tried to get to do your dirty work!

HERMAPHRODITE
Yeah, right!
Like I have the time and energy to try and seduce every guy in the palace to kill the Emperor!

SCAPULA
I for one can attest to the fact that you could...
(*sharing this with CARRYONUS and the audience*)
Her energy and stamina are amazing...it's like being with a wolverine in heat!

HERMAPHRODITE
Oh, enough! The point is I couldn't have tried to get everyone in the palace to do my bidding...

CARRYONUS
That's right! Which is another point of contention with you isn't it?

SCAPULA
What do you mean by that, Samsonite?

CARRYONUS
Before you were brought to the palace, 'Dite...what was your life like back in Greece?

HERMAPHRODITE
(*her dander up*)
I was the daughter of a wealthy wine & cheese merchant, if it's any of your business...I was going to inherit all! And I was engaged to marry a Prince of Moesia!

SCAPULA
(*half-aloud, to himself*)
Moesia? Sounds like one of those shows on the WB!

CARRYONUS
(*to SCAPULA*)
Try to stay in this time period, knucklehead.
(*back to HERMAPHRODITE*)
So, you were in line to be a princess?
And so all this bowing and scraping must really irk you, huh?
That sounds like a pretty solid motive for wanting to eliminate the cause of all your grief...namely the Emperor. With him out of the way, you'd probably stand a pretty good chance of being set free...seeing how you and the Empress don't get along very well.

{*Enter EMPRESS CHIANTI and MAXIMUS who carries a plate of fruit*}

CHIANTI
(*obviously a little tipsy and plucking off a few grapes from the tray MAXIMUS is holding*)
Who doesn't get along with me, noble brute!?
I am the most con...con...con-genitalia person I know!

MAXIMUS
That's congenial, my dear Empress, congenial...
Try to stop thinking about those eunuchs for a few minutes, won't you!

HERMAPHRODITE
This little hairy pip-squeak is trying to pin the Emperor's death on me! He is trying to imply that because of my past, I'm dissatisfied with my current station and that you and I are bitter enemies!

CHIANTI
(*stumbling over to her*)
But isn't that the truth!?
Since the first day that Cincinnatus brought you here...you and I have been enemas!!

MAXIMUS
Enemies, you drunken hussy...enemies!

CARRYONUS
(*kneeling once again before the nobility*)
All hail to thee, Queen of Roman Flotsam! I lay prostrate and bare before your imprudent Greatness!

HERMAPHRODITE
(*giving him a whack to the head*)
Aww, knock it off, will ya! Nobody wants to see your bare prostate!

CHIANTI
(*pushing HERMAPHRODITE away from the kneeling CARRYONUS*)
Leaf...(*hic*) Leaf...(*hic*) Leave him alone! If he wants to bare it...I wanna see it!

SCAPULA
Oh, enough of this!
(*pulling CARRYONUS to his feet*)
You barbarian, please refrain from your bowing and scraping...Our inebriated Empress and her equally besotted Senator may not be able to see through your thinly veiled derisive comments, but some of us around here are a lot more smarter than they are dumb...

HERMAPHRODITE
Nicely phrased, Scap'...Very well put.
I'm sure none of us are gonna match wits with the likes of you.

SCAPULA
Thank you, my dear 'Dite! It's nice to be finely appreciated...
And besides, my hirsute ruffian, your insipid salutations are not only very bad insults, but they only serve to heighten the Empress's already throbbing libido.

MAXIMUS
(*aside to audience*)
Tell me about it...
She hasn't been this bad since the Theater of Pompeii extended their run of Oh, Calcutta!

HERMAPHRODITE
(*walking over to CARRYONUS*)
Okay, since you obviously wanna play detective here, Shaggy...
(*pointing at CHIANTI and MAXIMUS*)
Why not accuse these two, huh? They got pretty good motives for wanting the Emperor dead!

CARRYONUS
Really? Wait a minute...Does everyone here in Rome have a motive?
Was everyone in Rome out to assassinate the Emperor?

CHIANTI
(*finally sobering...a little*)
It's ancient Rome, you barbaric bonehead!
If you don't have a motive, you're out of fashion...you know like the song says:

(*breaking into a funky '70's riff*)
"They smile in your face, all the time they wanna take your place, the Backstabbers...!"

MAXIMUS
All right, all right...calm down, Aretha!
We're trying to solve a heinous crime here...not 'boogie on down' on Soul Train!!

SCAPULA
Good one, Senator. Nice use of your superior diplomatic skills...

MAXIMUS
Uppa yours, Soldier Boy!
But to answer your question, Carryonus...I for one am not afraid to expose myself!
That's right! I did have a motive to want the Emperor dead...or at least executed.
He was my older brother, and as children he always got all the attention...
Julius conquered Gaul! Julius captured Egypt! Julius can conjugate Latin!
It was sickening!
So I vowed once I had achieved a seat in the Forum, that I would do all in my power to prove what a real ignoramus my brother really was!

CHIANTI
(*chiming in again*)
Yep. Thass right.
I fer one can surely attest to that...He surely was an igno...(*hic*) an igno...(*hic*) an ass.

HERMAPHRODITE
Easy, Empress...you're gonna strain something.
(*showing her to the pillows*)
Have a seat until your next line, okay? Good girl.

CARRYONUS
So...you harbored deep resentment for your brother...
How exactly were you planning on getting rid of him?

CHIANTI
(*jumping up before HERMAPHRODITE can stop her*)
I can answer that one!
(*spinning on HERMAHPRODTIE*)
Back off, Greasy! It's my next line!
'Sides, I haven't gotten the chance to talk about my motive yet...and it's a good one too...I'm real proud of it! Yep, ol' Senator Quick & Limp over there...him and me had it all worked out! See...seein's how I didn't really like the Emperor all that much...He was pretty lousy in the lovin' department... (*to audience member*) unlike you Stud-muffin (*sotto voce*) call me... Where was I? Oh, yeah...So Ol' Minimal Maximus and I had seen to it that all them other Senators over at the Forum...what a bunch of dried up old stiffs, they are, huh? (*to the same audience member*) Unlike you Stud-muffin (*sotto voce*) call me...

SCAPULA
Would you please put your hormones in check and get on with it!

CHIANTI
(*a little hurt, but responding with drunken intuitiveness*)
Hey...you wanna talk about hormones... (*pointing to HERMAPHRODITE*)
You go talk with little Miss "I Dream of Jeannie" over there!

MAXIMUS
Oh, nevermind...let me finish what she is trying to say...

CHIANTI
(*now the 'mean' drunk rears its ugly head*)
Aw, stuff it, Senator Second Fiddle...you couldn't explain your way out of a wet papyrus sack!

CARRYONUS
(*trying desperately to restore order*)
Okay, that's it!! Everybody to a neutral corner!
We only got time enough for one murder during this evening!
Now, before the Orgy out there gets concerned that the Emperor hasn't put in an appearance yet. Can we please get back to trying to figure out exactly what happened...so we all don't end up victims of a howling blood-thirsty mob?

SCAPULA
(*siding with him*)
Yes, the Barbarian is right!
Let us finally put an end to this confusion and mayhem and hand the mob a suitable scapegoat...that's all they want anyway, someone they can pin all their pent up guilt and frustrations on...
(*leaning over to HERMAPHRODITE, hoping to impress her*)
I studied the Psychology & Philosophy of Crowds under Asinineus the Corpulent you know...

HERMAPHRODITE
That doesn't surprise me...a fat ass teaching a fat head!

MAXIMUS
(*pointing at SCAPULA's backside*)

Shouldn't that be the other way around...?

CHIANTI
Oh, right! Like you got room to talk Maximus Density!!

HERMAPHRODITE
Wait, wait, wait...we still haven't gotten around to figuring this situation out yet.
Look, Empress, try to stay coherent for a few minutes and tell us what your motive for wanting the Emperor knocked off is...or was, now that he is. Is that right?

CARRYONUS
Close enough. Come on, your Mightiness...what was your motive?

CHIANTI
As I was saying before I was so rudely interrupted...
(she leans over to the same audience member she picked out earlier)
You're a big strong strapping buck, aren't you, Stud-muffin? (sotto voce) call me...
But seriously...I wanted the old goat bumped off because he was paying more attention to that stupid horse instead of me!
(*dropping character just for a second*)
...I could swear I've said that in another show...

SCAPULA
All right, it is well known the Emperor had a fondness for his horse...
But is that a strong enough motive for wanting the Emperor dead? Are you sure there isn't anything else we should know about, your highness?
(*getting right up in her face, accusingly*)

You wouldn't be harboring any political ambitions would...
Like, being the first Empress in Rome!!

CHIANTI
(*breathing on him as she replies*)
I am the First Empress of Rome, you twit!

SCAPULA
(*crumpling to floor due to her powerfully besotted breath*)
So...I...smell!

MAXIMUS
Oh, this is getting us nowhere!

CARRYONUS
True, Senator...so let's get back to you.
Being jealous of your brother's success is a pretty strong motive...
And you were also in a position to orchestrate the assassination...
The Empress pointed out that you had incited the other Senators to riot, causing them to attack the Emperor and do your dirty work for you!

MAXIMUS
That too is true...but you are forgetting one thing!
The Empress also pointed out as the Emperor stumbled about the room here like a epileptic porcupine, that due to that Oracle's prediction, he had all the nerve-endings sucked out of his entire body...
Even with all those daggers stuck in him, he could feel no pain and would've probably lingered on for weeks before noticing any ill effects!

HERMAPHRODITE
Yeah, so what's your point?
That still would've accomplished your goal...

MAXIMUS
Ah, but it would've given the little weasel enough time to figure out who had gotten the other Senators all riled up and I would've sent to the Coliseum as lion bait!
So...it wasn't a very good plan, now was it!

CHIANTI
(*giggling drunkenly*)
Couldn't have said better myself, doofus!

MAXIMUS
Who asked you!
If it hadn't been for you I wouldn't be in this position!

CHIANTI
Thass fer sure...I woulda made ya get on all fours!!! HAH!!
(*starting to move about the room in an inebriated dance*)
Whoo-hoo!! Bring on the dancing eunuchs and towel boys

HERMAPHRODITE
(*pulling the Empress back to her chair*)
Okay...I think someone needs a little Betty Ford moment.
Have a seat and lay off the St. Paulie Girl, will ya?
You're making us look bad...

MAXIMUS

Well let's forget about me for a moment...what about the dear General over there, what are his reasons for wanting the Emperor killed

SCAPULA

(*picking himself up*)
Why, I had none!
I was the Emperor's right hand, his military commander and truest friend!

HERMAPHRODITE

Please! He wanted the Emperor dead because of me...with Cincinnatus dead he thought he had a shot at getting into my wine cellar, if you get my drift.

CARRYONUS

Oh, I see...the oldest story in the book: the battle-hardened soldier in love with the Emperor's concubine.

HERMAPHRODITE

I don't know what storybooks you been reading pal, but there ain't nuthin' hard about ol' Scap!

SCAPULA

Lies...I tell you lies!
Perhaps I am not as firm as I once was, but that is hardly a reason for wanting to assassinate the Emperor! If I truly wanted him dead, I would have surrounded the city with my legions and demanded his head!

CARRYONUS
Geez, doesn't anybody around here do their own dirty work!?!

HERMAPHRODITE
Which brings us back to you, Thundar!
You seem pretty hung up on this "taking credit where credit is due" thing!
You admitted to me earlier that you had a plan to kill the Emperor with this poisoned dagger you had hidden behind these pillows!

CHIANTI
(*leaping up with a squeal*)
EEeeekk!!
There's a poisoned dagger in here!!??!!

SCAPULA
Wait a moment!
Did you say poisoned dagger? Hhhmmm.
Now, Maximus just said something about the Emperor's nervous ending...

HERMAPHRODITE
That's nerve-endings, Numskull...but that is a good point. The Emperor may not have been able to feel the daggers in him, but that wouldn't have stopped him from being poisoned!

SCAPULA
So then...it looks as though the Barbarian is the killer!
He was the one with poisoned dagger!

CARRYONUS
But how could I be the killer?

My dagger wasn't one of those sticking out his back!

SCAPULA
(*he has no reply for this so...*)
Oh well, then... shut-up!

MAXIMUS
(*patting SCAPULA on the shoulder*)
Nice try, old fellow.
Perhaps you should go sit next to the Empress...you know what they say:
(*makes a drinking motion with his hand*)
"Great minds think alike!"

CHIANTI
(*winking at SCAPULA*)
Thass right, Soldier-boy...you bring them cute buns over here and sit on Momma's lap!!

HERMAPHRODITE
(*moving over next to CARRYONUS*)
Okay...okay.
Looks like it's up to you and me, Samson.
It's pretty obvious that these three are losing their grip on reality...

CARRYONUS
True...the upper class has never been able to handle disaster well.
All right, let's go through this one more time to see if we've covered everything.
Now, you 'Dite...your motive was a thorough loathing of the Roman class system, based on the fact that back in Greece you were royalty...

And having to serve these Roman Boobyheads had driven you to the edge.

HERMAPHRODITE
(*getting into this detective stuff now*)
Right.
And you Carryonus have secretly harbored a hatred for your Roman captors and would have done anything to be free again, correct?!

CARRYONUS
Right! And General Scapula, though he truly is one of Rome's most valiant defender's...
had also been concealing his own desire for power and fame, not to mention his lust for you, the Emperor's concubine. With the Emperor out of the way there would be nothing to stop him from claiming all of Rome as his property!

HERMAPHRODITE
And Empress Booze-hound over there...
She wanted the Emperor dead because of his lack of bedroom gymnastics, his unnatural affection for that horse of his and a desire to become Rome's first female leader!

CARRYONUS
Correct! And Senator Testicles...

MAXIMUS
TENTACLES!! TENTACLES!!

CARRYONUS
Whatever...
He had a deep-seated revulsion for his brother's success...

Which all stems from a lack of motherly affection, coupled with an Oedipus complex and an obsession with his lack of procreative stamina!

MAXIMUS
(*aside, apologizing*)
You have no idea the pressure I've been under!

CHINATI
Okay, great...
We got everyone's butt covered on the "I really wanna kill this guy" portion of the show...

HERMAPHRODITE
Right...
And we've narrowed it down to the poison as the killer's weapon of choice...
But, that still leaves us with opportunity...I mean, who actually had the chance to poison him?

MAXIMUS
Yes, and if he wasn't killed with a poisoned dagger...then what weapon was used!?!

CHINATI
(*reaching for the grapes*)
Maybe the old fart ate something that disagreed with him…

MAXIMUS
(*grabbing them away from her*)
Your Highness!! These might be the weapon we're looking for!

HERMAPHRODITE
Or the wine! Remember he took a drink as he was stumbling around the room...!!

CARRYONUS
Well, I think I've got a pretty good idea of who the murderer is, but (*to customers*) maybe you folks have probably got theories of your own. Does anyone have any questions for our suspects? Let's start the questioning with Empress Chianti.
(*pause*)
Any questions for Senator Maximus?
(*pause*)
How about Hermaphrodite, any questions for her?
(*pause*)
Any questions for General Scapula?
(*pause*)
And last but not least, myself, does anyone have any questions for me?
Okay folks, now that the questioning is over with, it's time for you to solve this mystery. Find that sheet of paper inside your program marked Detective Sheet. Now here's how to fill them out...
Write down the name of the person whom you think killed our dear Emperor.
Then write down why, and be as specific as possible, because the one who comes closest to the right answers gonna win some nice prizes, okay? After that, if you would all be so kind to flip the sheet over and fill out the little questionnaire on the back, we'd appreciate it.
If you want to know about upcoming shows we might be having be sure to include your address and zip code and we'll add you to our mailing list. That will help us to keep bringing you more quality, educational programming like the one you've been watching!

And most important of all, don't forget to sign your name…you can't win a prize if we don't know the name of the person who won it!
We'll be back to collect those sheets in a moment.

{The Cast exits}

END ACT TWO

ACT THREE

{The third act opens, as did the first and two, with a flare of dramatic Hollywood Epic music, followed by a blaring of trumpets. SCAPULA, MAXIMUS, CHIANTI, and HERMAPHRODITE then enter and take up positions around the stage facing each other. EMPRESS CHIANTI should place herself fairly close to the "stud-muffin" she picked out in Act Two}

SCAPULA

All right, so where's the Samsonite...he said before we adjourned earlier, that he had a good idea which one of us was the one who murdered the Emperor.

MAXIMUS

He said he needed to check something in the kitchatorium, said he some questions for the cooks there...

SCAPULA

(*with a snort of derision*)

Well, that seems pretty suspicious to me...Why announce you know who the killer is, and then disappear!? Seems to me as if he was trying to buy time for his getaway!

HERMAPHRODITE

Take it easy, will ya... (*glancing down*)
You might wanna tuck your Erector Set back in...It's hanging out all over the place.

{While SCAPULA checks his toga, enter CARRYONUS running quickly -- He should also be carrying a set of shackles or chains to be used shortly}

CARRYONUS
(*enters quickly, takes center stage and gives another of his homeland's salutes*)
GREETINGS ONCE AGAIN, CONCUBINES, CAPTORS AND WINE SODDEN NOBLES!!

ALL
WILL YOU STOP DOING THAT!!

CHIANTI
(*still quite drunk, to her 'stud-muffin'*)
Hey...if he does that one more time, I want you to jump up and kick his Asia Minor!!

SCAPULA
Please, your highness...can we just get this over with! I want to get back to the orgy!

HERMAPHRODITE
I don't think anybody out there is interested in seeing the Decline of your Roman Empire!

MAXIMUS
Yes, get on with it, Samsonite! Or perhaps, We, should get on with it!
Your motive seems to be the strongest...eh, slave!? With the Emperor dead you would be free to return to your homeland...and free to start the U. S. S. R. Rebellion!!

CARRYONUS
What!?! You mean, you've known all along...!!! No matter...

But know this...I did not murder the Emperor!

SCAPULA

A fine thing to say, now that you are caught, you treacherous savage!
And to think I trusted you!!!

MAXIMUS

Yes, and a good thing you have brought those chains! Too bad they will be used to seal your doom...

CARRYONUS

(*he whips it out...his dagger I mean*)
All right!! Back off you soft, hairless Roman scum!

HERMAPHRODITE

Hey!! I'm Greek!

MAXIMUS

(*pulling CHIANTI close to him*)
Protect me! He's a mad killer!

CHIANTI

Hands off, Limpy! I got stud-muffin here to protect!
(*sotto voce*) After the show...call me...!!

CARRYONUS

(*taking charge once again*)
Put it in check, Empress...I got some news for you.
The rebellion I was planning with the U. S. S. R. has already begun!

Even now, all the slaves in Rome are rising up and taking over!
Soon the entire city will be ours!

SCAPULA
But... but how? I mean...Why?
If you're not the killer...why make such an outrageous announcement!?!

MAXIMUS
Because he's a stage hog, that's why!

HERMAPHRODITE
Wait a minute...you mean you were planning on assassinating the Emperor...and that was the signal for the insurrection to start, right?!

CHIANTI
Ooooh, if there's one thing I do love; it's a good insurrection...!

MAXIMUS
As if we didn't know that already!!

SCAPULA
So...you've begun the rebellion...but it will still go down in history as a mystery!
We have not been able to figure out who slew the Emperor!

CARRYONUS
Oh, I wouldn't bet on that, General.
If you remember...we had deduced that Cincinnatus had not died from his multiple stab wounds...but rather from some sort of ingested poison.

HERMAPHRODITE
Right! It had to be either the grapes or the wine!

CARRYONUS
That's correct, 'Dite! I ruled out the grapes early on...because The Empress and the Senator were eating them when they came in at the top of Act Two. Since neither of them is showing any sign of ill effects, it is natural to assume that the grapes are clean!

SCAPULA
(*indicating the surrounding restaurant*)
Well, they'd better be! Or the National Health Board will be all over this place!

MAXIMUS
Thank you, General Anachronism...this is supposed to be Ancient Rome, remember!?!

HERMAPHRODITE
So, if the grapes are okay... Then...it had to be the wine!

CHIANTI
That's what I always say...
How did he get in my bed? It had to be the wine!

CARRYONUS
Would someone please get her under control!
That's right...the wine. Now we all had access to the pitcher of wine that 'Dite brought in.
I myself am responsible for guarding the wine cellars, I could have poisoned it then...

SCAPULA
Aha! So you admit it!

MAXIMUS
But wait...I could have poisoned the wine, because I was the one who ordered it from those Etruscan wine merchants and was the one who saw it delivered to the wine cellar...

SCAPULA
Aha! So then you admit it!

HERMAPHRODITE
But I could've also been the one to have tainted the wine...I carried it up from the wine cellar...
I could've poisoned it then!

SCAPULA
(*a little unsure this time*)
So you then...you admit it?!

CHIANTI
Hold on a second, kids...I coulda intoxicated that wine too...I'm the one that poured it from the kegs into the pitchers...I coulda slipped in a dangerous poison then!

SCAPULA
(*a little unsure this time*)
Aha! So you then...Wait a minute! You can't all admit to it!
I did it! I poisoned the wine!

CARRYONUS
I knew we could trip him up!
If there's one thing I know about the General, it's that he's always taking credit for other people's exploits!

SCAPULA
But this time it's true! I really am the one who poisoned the wine! I did it on the road this past week! I'm the one who was responsible for picking it up from the Etruscan wine merchants, and delivering it to the wine cellar. I slipped the poison in between Bologna and Rome!

CHIANTI
I thought lettuce and tomato came between bologna and Rome...

CARRYONUS
Well, as you pointed out, General...it will go down in history as a mystery...an anonymous assassination on the eve of a great rebellion...

SCAPULA
Oh, yeah? (*he suddenly points behind CARRYONUS*) Hey...what the heck is that!?!
(*he leaps forward and grabs the poisoned knife away from the Samsonite*)
Hah! Yourselves! Who's got the knife now, eh!? Who's gonna write the history books now, eh!?

MAXIMUS
Uh, general... you're holding it the wrong way.

SCAPULA
(*glancing down and seeing that he is grasping the blade, not the handle*)
Oh, shit.

{*SCAPULA crumples to the floor, dead*}

MAXIMUS
You know...I think that's the first time he has ever done anything right...

HERMAPHRODITE
Okay...so we caught the assassin and solved the mystery... But we still got two other things to take care of...

CHIANTI
(*moving about quickly the room, caressing as many men as possible before MAIXMUS stops her*)
Only two? Heck...I could think of five or six things to take care of...
(*sotto voce*) After the show...call me...!!

MAXIMUS
(*pulling her out of the room*)
Come on, your highness...Leave the poor customers alone now... We've got to get back to the orgy...before all those rebellious slaves eat up all the cheese!

SFX CUE

MUSIC CUE:
EVERYBODY WANTS TO RULE THE WORLD

{*MAXIMUS and CHIANTI exit*}

HERMAPHRODITE
Tell me, Samsonite...now that your rebellion is under way...
You got room for an ex-Grecian Slave girl in your New World Order?

CARRYONUS
(*takes her arm-in-arm*)
Well, you know what they say..."Every Mauritanian Wants to Rule the World!"

{*HERMAPHRODITE and CARRYONUS exit as the song* **Everybody Wants to Rule the World** *plays*}

THE END

"Double O Zero's Day of Doom!"

Or

THE WORLD IS *MY* OYSTER CRACKER, BUCKO!

By
David J. Fielding
Copyright © 2011

SETTING

All of the action of this spy vs. spy Comedy-Mystery takes place in the vast underground lair of NIGEL JAXX on a remote volcanic island somewhere in the Pacific Ocean, at approximately 7:45pm on June 14th in the year 1964.

~~~~~~~~~~~~~~~~~~

CHARACTERS

Nigel Flapsmith "Flap" Jaxx
– An Eastern European Evil mastermind, multi-billionaire and space nut

Nigel Jaxx has been a thorn in the world's side pretty much since he could learn to walk and talk. Raised somewhere in Eastern Europe by a secret society of megalomaniacal beatniks and creepy circus criminals, Jaxx spent his childhood preparing to take over the world. He has been fascinated by space and the possibility of ruling the planet from an orbiting space station. He made his billions by offering novelty items in the backs of comic books – hey, you'd be surprised how many people will pay a $1 for a pair of fake 3-D glasses. Jaxx has traded wits and bullets with Jason Bondo and several occasions, and nothing would make him happier than to finally put that no good, goody-two-shoes on ice – permanently!

Jason Bondo, Agent 00-Zero
– The United Kingdom's best super-agent – regardless of what that other 00 guy has done

Jason Bondo is a five-time decorated British military man, recruited by MI6 and trained in all sorts of really nifty spy-like stuff – suave techniques to impress the ladies, sweet judo moves and access to all sorts or really neato gadgets and gizmos. Throughout his years as a super-agent, he has undergone rigorous physical and mental preparation in order to prepare him for his various missions. He speaks seven languages, is skilled in seventeen different hand-to-hand techniques and well versed in the art of seduction. Bondo has come into contact with each of the villains in tonight's show, thwarting each of them in turn and earning their undying hatred. Because of his many exploits dealing with these nefarious criminal minds, Jason has survived just about every known way to kill a person… and there are some who say that nothing can kill him!

FOO YOO
- Mysterious Asiatic "King of the Underworld" & Reality TV show producer

The enigmatic and darkly dangerous Foo Yoo is a name that generates fear and respect – at least in the six or seven people that have heard of him. The world has yet to know of this lesser known nephew of the evil and insidious Fu Manchu – one of the greatest villains of all time – so Foo's got some pretty big pointy slippers to fill. But, he has already put into motion plans to take over the world – the reality TV show! He has come to Jaxx's island lair to either get Jaxx to pitch a series, or join him as producer – or at least to give him a small loan. What would really put Foo's name on the map though would be if he could rid the world of its greatest spy Jason Bondo – and that's just what he'll do, you watch, he will!

SHEILA BUSHYWOOD
– Australian billionaire heiress, big game hunter and also a genius of high finance

Shelia Bushywood is well known throughout the business world as one of the most cut-throat and cruel ladies of high finance. She has crushed hundreds on her way to the top and won't stop until she controls all the world's financial markets. In her spare time she enjoys hunting big game – rabbits, squirrels and all sorts of other ugly rodents. They remind her, she says, of her business competitors – small, wiry and easy to squash. There's only one thing that stands in her way of total world domination – Jason Bondo and nothing would make her happier than to finally put that busy body, rotten stinking super-agent six feet under – and don't think she won't do it either!

ALEXIS SOPHIA VULVAE
- American film and TV star, of Royal Russian descent and a software expert – computer software (get your mind out of the gutter, sheesh)*!*

Alexis Vulvae is famous – super famous, like she's really, really, really famous – yeah, that kind of famous. Billboards, magazine ads, TV commercials – you name it, she's done them all. She's taken Hollywood by storm – so why not the whole world!? She's gonna use all her feminine charms to bend the planet to her will – her minions are busy developing a software program that's decades ahead of its time. This program will turn all of us into her own personal mindless slaves – worshiping Alexis Vulvae as the one and only! The only wrinkle in her plan is – you guessed it, that pesky British spy Double O-Zero, Jason Bondo and nothing would make her happier than to see him cut out of the picture – once and for all!

FUN FACTS

NIGEL JAXX – His early years are shrouded in mystery and but one rumor that has been widely circulated is that he was part of the Nazi top secret space program and in fact was blasted into space in late 1948, more than a decade before Yuri Gagarin. Refuting experts claim that Jaxx merely fell off a launching pad and cracked his skull… and that his "trip into space" was merely time spent in a psychiatric ward.

SHEILA BUSHYWOOD – almost a legend in her home country of Australia, the infamous 'Sure-shot Shelia' is the subject of great controversy given her penchant for treating her business dealings like big game hunts. Literally. She takes her rivals out into the bush and hunts them until they concede or she loses them… and she never loses them.

FOO YOO – Not much is known about this new player on the stage of world domination. What little intel is known about him is that he hails from some unknown region in Asia, that he dresses in very ornate robes and Oriental-style clothes, has a entourage that numbers just over a hundred and excels at the game of Checkers. He has lately been seen visiting a number of producers and studio heads in Hollywood, talking with them about his top secret television show idea. Whatever it is, experts fear it may involve nefarious plans to take over the world… or at least Cleveland.

ALEXIS VULVAE – This beautiful and charismatic goddess of the silver screen has conquered not only the advertising and entertainment venues, she's also done a lot of damage on the fashion and haute couture circuits as well. A driven, sensuous and demanding movie star, Alexis has gone through six hundred and twelve personal assistants, four husbands and sixteen publicists – all because "they never really got me, you know? I mean, all I'm asking for is for people to just do and say what I want… is that so hard?" The movie magazines all call her the Black Widow… which surprisingly is a name she likes.

JASON BONDO – The highly decorated naval officer Commander Jason Bondo was recruited into MI6 in the middle 50's and trained in all manner of espionage, surveillance and counter-intelligence protocols. He is an expert in armed and unarmed combat, a snappy dresser, has a weakness for Singapore Slings and has written a best-selling book, "Women of the World and How to Get Any of Them to Kiss You".

PRODUCTION NOTES

The following notes are given for each cast to consider using so that they may best convey the look and feel that the production aims to achieve. Naturally each cast will have their own ideas and concepts about how best to present the atmosphere and ambience of an evil genius' underground lair on a volcanic island.

COSTUMES – Costumes should be as complete as possible and should give the audience information and clues about each of the characters. For inspiration please look at films such as ***Dr. No***, ***Casino Royale (1967)*** and the ***Austin Powers*** trilogy.

- NIGEL JAXX – should be dressed as pretty close to the outfit worn by Hugo Draxx – the villain from the Moonraker movie. Beige or blue Nehru jacket buttoned up to the mandarin collar. The actor's hair should either be slicked back, bald or wearing an obvious bald-head wig. Black pants and black shoes finish the outfit. Perhaps adding the eyepatch ala the James Bond villain Largo. The "space" version of this outfit is simply a plastic dome that JAXX wears.

- JAMES BONDO – should be dressed in either a tuxedo – all black or white jacket, black pants. Your pretty standard James Bond rip-off.

- FOO YOO – should be dressed as close to a Fu Manchu type as possible – ornate oriental long jacket, Chinese box hat, wicked long press on nails and the requisite Fu Manchu moustache

- **SHEILA BUSHYWOOD** – should be dressed in the same vein as Frau Farbissina or Rosa Kleb – masculine and tough. Dark jacket, slacks and dark pointed shoes or boots. Alternatively, she can be dressed in either military or Big Game Hunter garb. The hair style should be severe and mannish. In contrast to the manly garb, she wears an ornate poison ring on one hand.

- **ALEXIS VULVAE** – should be dressed as sexy and alluring as possible, very much along the lines of Nancy Sinatra, Jill St. John or Raquel Welch – she should contrast strongly with BUSHYWOOD – one is masculine, the other very feminine.

PLAYING SPACE – In addition to the regular set up materials (*fun facts, pencils and WhoDunnit Cards*) the acting area should have three spots on different walls or support beams where a panel of fake buttons can be placed – this panel can be as simple as a drawing of buttons or as ornate as the cast can make it – a cheap plastic socket plate with bright colored wooden circles glued on it will also work – all depending on the company budget, of course. Anything you can do to give the playing space the more atmosphere the better you can use it to your advantage and to draw the audience into playing along.

ACT ONE

SFX CUE*

{The show begins with a short announcement, played over the intercom/speaker system}

VOICE OVER

Ladies and Gentlemen, our production of **Double O-Zero's Day of Doom** will begin shortly, but before we begin, please note that any stereotypes, horribly racially insensitive characterizations and just plain bad acting are all meant to be for fun and hilarity -- and in no way are meant as a slight to any race, creed or color. Heck, if they can get away with it in the Austin Powers movies, so can we… and without any further ado –

*MUSIC

{dramatic stinger music, reminiscent of the James Bond opening gun-barrel sequence}

(*overly dramatic voice*)
DOUBLE O-ZERO's DAY OF DOOM!

*MUSIC

*{dramatic music segues into the "evil lair theme" of NIGEL JAXX (if you have the access to it – the main theme from the video game **EVIL GENIUS** it is perfect); the evil genius NIGEL JAXX enters, wearing the 'space' version of his outfit ** see costume notes}*

NIGEL JAXX
(*marching to the center of the room and spinning to face the entrance as FOO YOO enters, then removing his helmet*)
Welcome... welcome to my island lair, Foo Yoo.

FOO YOO
(*looking about*)
Impressive. You have created perfect hideaway...

NIGEL JAXX
I am not hiding from anyone, Foo... on the contrary...
I have allowed my minions to leak the exact location of this island to every known authority in the world...

FOO YOO
(*aghast*)
Are you crazy person? You give away location of secret lair?

NIGEL JAXX
Indeed, Foo. This is what separates me from you – I am a true evil genius... I fear no one.
You on the other hand tremble under your expensive oriental robes at the mere mention of the forces of good...

FOO YOO
Untrue, Jaxx. Do not believe fearful demeanor – it is ruse.
To appear weak, is to reveal strength.
(*he unfolds his arms to show that he is holding a small pistol hidden his huge sleeves*)
As you can see, tables have turned.

NIGEL JAXX

Ah. An excellent use of misdirection and subterfuge, Foo; and you would be in a position to do me harm... If that were indeed a real gun.

FOO YOO

(*smiles evilly*)

Is real enough. But bullets not best choice for killing.
I have more dastardly surprise for true nemesis... Jason Bondo.

NIGEL JAXX

(*smiles, then laughs*)

Very good, my friend! I knew when I invited you here that I had chosen well.
Please, have a seat... can I offer you some refreshment while we await the others?

FOO YOO

(*he doesn't move, and returns the gun to the hidden pocket in his sleeve*)

Perhaps I stand... see what unfolds.
Who else has accepted honorable invitation?

NIGEL JAXX

Two of like mind as you and I, my friend... the very wealthy and very formidable Frau Shelia Bushywood and the very beautiful and very deadly Ms. Alexis Vulvae.

{*as he mentions them by name, the two women enter into the room, each giving the other the once over before separating behind FOO, who has not seen them enter*}

FOO YOO

Ah... The Warhound and the Dragon Lady.

BUSHYWOOD
Watch who you're calling names, lispy.

ALEXIS
Darn tootin'! You're lucky I really dig that outfit you are wearing, Hop-sing; otherwise you'd be dead for calling me a dog…

BUSHYWOOD
(*giving her a look*)
I think he was calling me a dog and you a snake…

ALEXIS
Oh yeah!?
(*really angry now, steps up to FOO and grabs him by the collar, lifting him up onto his tip-toes*)
Snake, huh? Got anything else smart to say before I end your life, little man!?

FOO YOO
I love you in *Dame is Murder*! You my favorite for Oscar!

ALEXIS
(*her one weakness, flattery*)
Aw! That's so sweet!
(*she drops him, compliments his outfit*)
Where did you get this, it's divine! Who designed it?

BUSHYWOOD
AHEM!
If the fun and games are over? … Alright, Jaxx… you got us here… what's the plan?

NIGEL JAXX
Simple my dear, Fräulein …
We kill Jason Bondo.

FOO YOO
Not so simple, Herr Jaxx.
(*he moves away from ALEXIS, and examining his long fingernails*)
British Intelligence train agents well… He extremely hard to kill.

BUSHYWOOD
Too right! Six weeks ago I had him cornered in the jungles of Sumatra, but he managed to weasel out of the trap I'd set for him!

ALEXIS
I had him two years ago in Las Vegas, Nevada… had him dead to rights…
My gun was pressed against his chest, and he still managed to escape!
(*she stomps her foot in frustration*)

FOO YOO
I meet him only once… at Katz Deli in New York City.
He order corned beef on rye… and leave me with bill.
Very irritating.

(*they all stare at FOO as though he is from another planet*)

NIGEL JAXX
We have all suffered at the hands of Jason Bondo… my question for each of you is this – if I provide you with the opportunity… how would you kill Agent Double-O Zero?

(*each of the evil geniuses trade eye contact, evaluating each other*)

BUSYWOOD

Don't know about the rest of you, but I gots me a nice little surprise for 'im.
Just got to get in close to 'im… and then, a little puff and poof, no more Mr. Bondo.

ALEXIS

So you're gonna blow on him and that's gonna kill him? Please… you got one thing right though, the only way to kill him is to get in close, real close… kill him with kisses you might say…

FOO YOO

Most disturbing image ever. But must agree… getting close is key to killing Agent Bondo… must be like kitten… (*he acts this out in an amusing way*)… Silent and swift, look to be playing… bat the string! Bat the string! (*he indicates his fingernails*) But claws are deadly!

NIGEL JAXX

(*is not amused*)

And this is why none of us evil genius's get the respect we deserve!
Though I cannot agree with your methods, I think I know what each of you is planning… but mine will be the one that puts an end to Agent Bondo, once and for all!

BUSHYWOOD

Oh yeah? So what's your big plan, eh? Gonna trick him into using one of your fancy gizmos I bet! How lame… how many times have you tried that Jaxx? 10? A hundred?
He ain't gonna fall for the same ol' tricks, pea-brain!

NIGEL JAXX
Shut up!
(*getting control of himself*)
No matter what our methods are my friends… we will all get our shot (*he titters*) at Jason Bondo.
(*he pulls a communicator out of his pocket and taps a few buttons*)
Ah, punctual as usual…
Our slippery spy friend has just entered the complex…

BUSHYWOOD
He's here?

****MUSIC CUE –
DRAMATIC STING**

{*bounding in through the entrance comes the hero, JASON BONDO - He's cool, suave and hip.
In his hand is his signature pistol, a sleek and slick Walther-PPK - or something like that.
He smiles, cool and sure of himself*}

JASON BONDO
Your security system is a joke, Jaxx.
Getting into your secret underground lair was as easy as unhooking Ms. Vulvae's wonderbra… right sugarlips?
(*his gun tracking back and forth between his enemies*)
Nice of you to gather all these notorious villains in one place, Jaxx… you sure you aren't working for MI6 as a double agent?

{*the others gasp and curse, turning their attention toward JAXX*}

NIGEL JAXX

Nice try, Herr Bondo... but you are mistaken. While you have managed to gain the upper hand in previous encounters... it is you who is at a disadvantage here.

JASON BONDO

(*looks about, unphased*)

I'm the one with the gun, superior marksmanship abilities and the drop on all of you... what puts me at a disadvantage?

{*NIGEL JAXX takes a single step toward a nearby wall or other prominent feature of the playing space – a beam/roof support, for example – the actor playing NIGEL JAXX should be aware of this moment in the show and should place himself according, anticipating the bit about to occur – alternatively he can use the controller he pulled from his pocket earlier*}

NIGEL JAXX

Only this – (*he presses the controller in his hand or an unseen button on the wall – if possible he should have concealed in his pocket a buzzer or noise maker that simulates some sort of electro-magnetic device has been triggered*) – your weapon is now useless, Agent Double O Zero – as might I point out, are all of the concealed weapons of my guests...

{*all of the others react to this –*

BONDO *tries to fire his gun, but it is useless, and clicks on empty chamber after empty chamber;*
ALEXIS *pulls a handgun out of her purse and tries to fire it – nothing;*
BUSHYWOOD *takes the gun out of her waist and again, the same result, nothing;*

FOO YOO removes the small gun from his sleeve and shoots it, only to produce an embarrassing dribble of water [his weapon should be a squirt gun obviously]

NIGEL JAXX begins to laugh, a giggle that turns to a guffaw that turns into a boisterous evil bellow – all of the others look at him for a beat and then yell}

ALL
Oh SHUT UP!

FOO YOO
You make gun dribble… no fair!

ALEXIS
Hey! What gives! This baby shoots genuine diamond bullets… where'd they go?

BUSHYWOOD
He's filled the room with some sort of electro-magnetic-dampening induction field… it's rendered all of our weapons ineffective!

JASON BONDO
Well played, Jaxx… but the games not over…

ALEXIS
Wait a minute… how can his electro-whats-it thingee turn my pretty diamond bullet pistol into just a hunk of junk? Diamonds ain't electro-magnetic or whatever!

FOO YOO
Close pie-hole! MY gun is leaking!

BUSHYWOOD
Yeah, keep your skirt on Ms. Thang.
So what now, Jaxx… you kill us all, that it?
You come up with this false invitation to kill Agent Double O-Zero, just as a way to get all of us here and take us out together? That ends your competition and your nemesis in one fell swoop!

NIGEL JAXX
(*who is still tittering a bit*)
Oh, my invitation to all of you is still very real, Fräulein Bushywood… I invited you here for a chance to eliminate the great Double O-Zero and believe me, Jason Bondo will not leave this island alive… but I have no plans to get rid of you or Foo or Ms. Vulvae…

BUSYWOOD
(*nonchalantly examining JAXX's space helmet ** important plot point – see ACT III*)
Then what's the kafuffle, Jaxx? What you got up your sleeve?

FOO YOO
He have arm up sleeve…

{*The others ignore FOO's nonsensical remark*}

JASON BONDO
Might as well reveal your plan, Jaxx…
If I'm going to die, explain away…

ALEXIS
Yeah, something tells me that killing off the super spy ain't all you got in the works…

NIGEL JAXX
Very well, since you insist I reveal my plan – which is a stereotypical plot device to clue the audience in on stuff that will be important later… (*all the cast members look about and tell the audience to pay attention*) … allow me to enlighten you as to my grand and glorious scheme.

{*NIGEL JAXX presses the panel on the wall or support beam once more and a soft music fills the air, a tropical music reminiscent of BALI HAI or ALOHA-OE, he then begins to walk to a chair that has been placed in the center and sits*}

FOO YOO
Have funny feeling… (*he looks about, counting the other players*)

ALEXIS
There's five of us, Foo… you can count to five, can't you?

FOO YOO
Whew! … Good thing there are not seven… me start to think we on Gilligan's Island…

BUSHYWOOD
(*angry at his idiocy*)
If this here gun were workin' I'd empty every last chamber into ya!

FOO YOO
(*sneering at BUSHYWOOD*)

Is no matter… have learned ancient martial art secret… I dodge bullet.

BUSHYWOOD
(*she clomps over to him*)
Oh yeah!?

FOO YOO
(*FOO assumes the fighting crane stance from* **The Karate Kid**)
Hiii-ya!

{*BUSHYWOOD stomps on FOO's foot and he hops about in pain – they then begin to chase each other about, eventually encircling BONDO, using him as a shield from each other - during this chase BONDO should sneeze at one point - **note this bit will be important in ACT II*}

NIGEL JAXX
Enough!
(*swiveling to face BONDO*)
You have been a thorn in our sides for many years, Mr. Bondo… you and I have traded wits on several occasions…

JASON BONDO
Twenty Two and three-quarters by my count, Jaxx…

ALEXIS
Three-quarters? Why didn't you finish the last one?

JASON BONDO
Let's just say Jaxx was a little… premature…

{*all of the others let out laughter at this*}

NIGEL JAXX
SHUT UP!
(*one of JAXX's eyes start to twitch*)

ALEXIS
Ooooh! You know they have ways to prevent that from happening…

FOO YOO
You need cream? I call Hong Kong for special Puffer Fish remedy…

BUSHYWOOD
In the outback we gots a cure for that ya know…just gotta wrestle a croc for it is all…

NIGEL JAXX
SHUT UP!
(*he slaps a hand over his twitching eye*)
It wasn't my fault… the wiring in the rocket was faulty!
NEVER MIND!
(*controlling himself*)
It doesn't matter… what matters is you are trapped here Mr. Bondo… trapped in this complex with four of the world's top evil geniuses… all who have plans to kill you.
(*the is a pause*)
And let me very plain… the one who kills Mr. Bondo… shall be declared the greatest villain of all time!

ALEXIS
You mean …!

NIGEL JAXX

Precisely!! Endorsement deals and unlimited ad revenue! Kill Jason Bondo and you win it all -- Power, fame and the Heavyweight Title Belt of Villainy!

{JAXX pulls out the title belt from beneath the chair – all the others oooh and ahhh
– and then all turn toward BONDO, murder in their eyes}

JASON BONDO

(*it starts to sink in this may be more serious than he thought*)
Heh … well, it's been good to see you Jaxx old chap… but unfortunately I have to dash… due to check in with MI6 in about half an hour, so I'll … uh, … just see myself out…

{he turns to exit but the others move to intercept, forcing him back toward the center of the room}

BUSHYWOOD

(*she pulls a big knife/machete out of her belt*)
You done ruined a lot plans of mine, you 'ave. And I'm mad as cut snake... so I'm gonna dice you up into and feed you to the sharks…

FOO YOO

(*he has revealed a long acupuncture needle and advances on BONDO, jabbing it menacingly*)
You stick me with bill in New York Deli!
Me short on cash and had to do dishes! I hate you for that!

ALEXIS

(*she has revealed a butterfly-knife strapped to her thigh*)
You distracted me with that kiss last time Jason… but not this time! I'm gonna slice you to ribbons!

JASON BONDO
(*looks about, readying himself to fight them all… but then he notices that JAXX hasn't moved*)
What about you, Jaxx? Got something sharp to use on me too? A letter opener? Maybe a pizza slicer?

{*JAXX doesn't answer*}

JASON BONDO
Jaxx?

ALEXIS
Hey, baldy (*or some funny remark about the characters look or dress*)… you ok?

FOO YOO
Refrain from performing marsupial!

BUSHYWOOD
You mean possum… Quit playing Possum.

FOO YOO
(*he is confused*)
That is what I said.

{*BONDO moves over to wear JAXX is sitting. JAXX is sitting upright in his chair, seemingly paralyzed – the expression on his face should be the same look of triumph as when he pulled out the Villain Belt, which is clutched in his 'frozen' or 'paralyzed hand*}

JASON BONDO
Nobody move! If my instincts are correct … and my instincts are always correct …
(*he winks at ALEXIS, who blushes*)
Jaxx has fallen victim to his own horrible traps. He's dead.

FOO YOO
You make joke. How he fall for trap we not know of… he had yet to reveal his master plan.

BUSHYWOOD
I hate to agree with the … (*she turns to FOO confused*) where are you from anyway? China? Japan? Korea?

FOO YOO
Ancient and Honorable birthplace of my Ancestors… (*wait for it*) Upper St. Clair.
(*or whatever community is familiar to the patrons watching the show*)

BUSHYWOOD
(*glares at FOO*)
You need to be punched… hard. Anyway, he's right.
Jaxx hadn't told us his master plan –
While killing you was pretty much what all of us wanted, all of us had … ulterior motives in the works…

JASON BONDO
(*thinking*)
That's true.
(*he moves about the body, examining it – then he addresses the others*)
So, let's see if I can shed some light on that point… or points considering there's more than one of you…

FOO YOO
(*looks about himself, confused*)
Only one of me… you need eyes checked.

ALEXIS
He means that… oh, never mind!
(*she grins alluring at BONDO*)
Go ahead sweet thing… stun us with your undercover spy stuff!

BUSHYWOOD
(*cannot believe her*)
Seriously? You are seriously one of the top evil geniuses?

ALEXIS
(*strikes a challenging yet sexy pose*)
That's right.
They don't call me the Black Widow fer nuthin'.

FOO YOO
You not Spider – you Snake; I call you that earlier.

ALEXIS
Oh yeah!?
(*repeating the earlier bit, steps up and grabs FOO by the collar, lifting him up onto his tip-toes*)
Call me a Snake, will ya?

FOO YOO
I love you in She Demon of Broadway!
You win Tony!

ALEXIS
(*her one weakness, flattery*)
Hey! I did win a Tony! That's so sweet of you to remember!
(*she drops him and fluffs her hair, FOO scurries away*)

JASON BONDO
If we can please get back to the matter at hand? Great. Now, as we have established, Jaxx had yet to reveal his master plan… (he looks about the room) madmen (he gets dark looks from the girls) and women, mad-women… always leave clues as to what their twisted minds are plotting…

FOO YOO
He wearing bubble on head earlier… maybe is clue…

BUSHYWOOD
It's not a bubble, bobble-head… it's a helmet. A space helmet.

JASON BONDO
(*he picks up the helmet and examines it*)
Hmmm. This design is pretty advanced… more advanced than either of the British or American space programs.

BUSHYWOOD
The British have a space program?

JASON BONDO
Of course. (*he gives her a look*) But, you know all about that… don't you Shelia?

BUSHYWOOD
(*flustered*)

I don't... don't know what you're talking about.

JASON BONDO

Oh, come now... you've got real estate and land holdings in Woomera, don't you Shelia?

ALEXIS

Woo-what?

FOO YOO

No, not Woo – Foo. Foo is name.

ALL

SHUT UP!

JASON BONDO

Woomera, South Australia... Or should I say, the Woomera Test Range. It's a restricted village in the outback; a testing ground for the joint British and Australia space rocket program.
Ms. Bushywood stands to make millions off her sale of the land in and around Woomera... that and she has her eye on stealing the research being conducted there...

ALEXIS

Who cares about some silly old rockets?

BUSHYWOOD

(*caught, but haughty about her plans*)
It's not the rockets, honey, it's the payload...

FOO YOO

Ooooh, I get joke!

(*he motions to the others*)
She make sexy joke… rocket… payload!

ALEXIS
(*still standing close by, tweaks FOO's ear, hard*)
Shut it.

BUSHYWOOD
Pretty good, Double O-Zero.
Not many people know about the nuclear capabilities of the space program at Woomera.

ALEXIS
(*feigning shock*)
Nuclear! How could you… That's just so…

BUSHYWOOD
(*filled with glee*)
Evil?
Yeah … I know! I can kill a lot of rodents with them things!

JASON BONDO
Don't act so surprised, Ms. Vulvae… you've got payload secrets yourself…

{*anticipating, they all spin on FOO expecting him to make some dumb crack – he looks at them, hurt*}

FOO YOO
What! She twist hard… I think I deaf in ear now!

ALEXIS
Yeah? So enlighten me, Jason...
What do I have to do with rockets and space programs or nuclear bombs?

FOO YOO
Nuclear bombs! Holy crow... those things are evil!

BUSHYWOOD
(*filled with glee*)
Yeah ... I know!

JASON BONDO
No interest in rockets or nuclear bombs, Alexis?
What about ... Operation Sunbeam?

ALEXIS
(*reacts with genuine shock*)
How did you ...!?

JASON BONDO
Las Vegas, Nevada... two years ago.

ALEXIS
(*her mouth drops open... but she smiles in admiration*)
Oh, you're good... you're very good!

FOO YOO
Oh, yeah? Well me not in on joke this time. What Operation Moonbeam?

ALEXIS
Sunbeam, you bonehead.
Operation Sunbeam was the last above ground nuclear test conducted by the US of A.
(*back to BONDO*)
And here all along I thought you were trying to foil my scheme to steal millions from the Stardust and MGM Grand…

JASON BONDO
I did if you remember … killed two birds with one stone that mission. Kept you from getting all the money and I foiled your secret attempt to steal Little Fella's payload.

FOO YOO
(*very confused*)
Little Fella… you make new sexy joke?

ALEXIS
(*swats at him, but he scampers away*)
Little Fella, you moron!
Little Fella was the name of the last Davy Crockett warheads… I should've known it was you…
(*she saunters over to BONDO*)
I guess I was just a little… distracted.

JASON BONDO
(*takes ALEXIS in his arms*)
I knew you were planning on stealing the rocket… waiting for the heat to die down and use it to blast the rocket into space to take out the MIDAS 9 satellite this year.
Destroying the satellite would effectively cause a media blackout of the Fall Florence Fashion Show – enabling you to corner the market, netting you millions.

{*BONDO dips her and they share a movie screen kiss – the other two groan and attempt to get the audience to sympathize with them*}

BUSHYWOOD
Ok, alright… enough with the Pashy stuff…

{*BONDO and ALEXIS separate, both a little drunk on the moment*}

ALEXIS
(*sotto voce, to the actor playing BONDO – breaking character*)
I'll give you my cell number backstage… call me, text, whatever… I'm easy…

FOO YOO
(*to audience member nearby*)
She real easy… even you get lucky…

BUSHYWOOD
So, you uncovered both mine and the trollop's schemes -- both involving rockets and nuclear warheads – what about the Drongo with the face fungus… (*they all look at her like she's speaking alien – then she points to FOO*) Him! Face fungus – whiskers!

ALL
Oh! Right… got it.

JASON BONDO
Yoo Foo…

FOO YOO
Foo Yoo!

JASON BONDO
Hey! This is a family show!

FOO YOO
No... is name. FOO YOO. Not Yoo Foo...

JASON BONDO
Oh. Ok.
(*slight pause*) Yoo-Hoo...

{*FOO throws up his hands*}

ALEXIS
Just get on with it!

JASON BONDO
We met in New York last year...

FOO YOO
(*explodes with anger*)
You owe me for corned beef sandwich, cheapskate!

JASON BONDO
Calm down... I may have stuck you with the bill, but what you're really angry about is the fiasco at Indian Point Energy Center on the Hudson River... Am I right?

FOO YOO
You bet your bippy! Plan was to steal nuclear rods... place them in rockets at Malta Test Site near Saratoga... bye-bye New York and bye-bye Katz Deli and stupid corned beef sandwich!

BUSHYWOOD
Pretty impressive, Double O-Zero... seems like you've managed to uncover all our dirty little secrets...

JASON BONDO
(*motions to JAXX*)
All but our friend here...
(*he picks up the helmet again*)
Jaxx was part of the SS top-secret rocket program during WWII... or at least that's what he claims... this helmet proves what I was sent here to investigate... Jaxx has a missile silo buried under the volcano and with it he plans to launch himself into space...

ALEXIS
Yeah, well if he had...
Good riddance I say, one less nutjob to compete with...

JASON BONDO
So you admit to killing him?

{*the others gasp*}

ALEXIS
You're crazy! I didn't kill him! What reason do I have?

JASON BONDO
(*still examining the helmet*)
Well, he's already successfully established a space station that is orbiting the planet...

{*the others gasp again – they can't believe it*}

FOO YOO
You crazy! If true - how come it not on news!?

JASON BONDO
The US and British governments didn't want to start a panic... and if you three had heard about it, there was bound to be a race to try and take it from him...

BUSHYWOOD
So -- you're saying one of us killed him, and had plans all along to steal a space station we had no idea existed... I take it back what I said earlier, you're an idiot.

FOO YOO
(*he busts out laughing*)
Heee-heee!
You get it wrong!
Big time super spy is so stupid...

ALEXIS
Have to agree there, darlin' seems like you really kinda screwed the pooch on this one... none of us knew about the space station... We don't even know if it's real or not!

BUSHYWOOD
Yeah, could be that was Jaxx's plan
– fake a space station to lure you down here to kill you, just like he said.
Jason Bondo wasn't going to leave this island alive!

FOO YOO
(*still laughing*)

Heee-heee!
You get it wrong!
Big time super spy is so stupid…

JASON BONDO
(*genuinely confused*)
Hmmm. I could've sworn…
Hold it a second… I'll prove to you the station exists.
(*he takes the helmet and positions it, ready to put it on*)
This helmet's got a radio attachment, my guess it's tuned to the space station's frequency…
All I have to is slip it on, open a radio channel and then you'll know the space station is real!

{*he takes the helmet and slips it over his head… he twiddles a few dials and then… begins choking! He gasps and struggles, makes a big show of it and then collapses on the floor… dead! JASON BONDO is dead! – There is a moment of stunned silence from the other three evil geniuses – and then suddenly NIGEL JAXX leaps up out of his chair, his evil laugh filling the room*}

ALL
AHHhhhh! You scared the life out of me! What the heck!

NIGEL JAXX
It worked! It worked! Jason Bondo is dead!

BUSHYWOOD
You sly dog!
You were shining us on weren't you!?

ALEXIS
(*kind of sad*)

Oh, wow... he's really dead!

FOO YOO
You pull fast one! You not dead – but fake it... What you use? Fugu poison? Cassava root?

NIGEL JAXX
**Patience friends, patience! I will reveal everything to you... but first, I must insist you accompany me to dinner. Eliminating one's nemesis creates quite a hunger. Let us eat and then I will reveal how I, Nigel Jaxx, have killed the world's greatest super spy!

{The CAST, taking JASON BONDO with them makes their exit –
*** It is possible that venues will want to run ACTS I and II back to back – if that is the case – use the following alternative scene instead of the exit to JAXX's dining room}*

NIGEL JAXX
**Patience friends, patience! I will reveal everything to you... but first if you would be so kind as to help me. There is nothing more satisfying, than to display one's trophies after a hard won competition – or hunt... am I right, Fräulein Bushywood?

BUSHYWOOD
Too right!

FOO YOO
What you need us to do?

{there should be a place designated by the cast during their familiarizing themselves with the playing space that they can use as JAXX's "trophy case". Basically it's an area between tables where the

actor playing JASON BONDO can be set and posed according to the next bit}

NIGEL JAXX
Please help me place the unfortunate Mr. Bondo on this display platform!

{They place him in a rather unflattering pose and then all take a step back to admire their handiwork - at this point the show can continue as ACT II}

END ACT ONE

ACT TWO

{If the show is performed with a break between ACTS I and II – use the following as the opening segment for the opening of ACT II:
After the break, there is a burst of dramatic music – the same 60's James Bond-esque sting used throughout the show - which then segues into a lounge piece in the same vein as ESQUIVEL (Surfboard or Sentimental Journey) or HERB ALBERT (Whipped Cream or The Casino Royale Theme) or BURT BACHARACH (The Look of Love or I'll Never Fall in Love Again) –
As the music plays, the CHARACTERS enter into the playing space guiding a stiff and apparently dead JASON BONDO to a place previously designated by the CAST as JAXX's "trophy display case"}

SFX CUE

BUSHYWOOD
Gotta hand it to ya, Jaxx…
Your boys in the cook house sure know how to throw an honest to goodness barbie!

ALEXIS
You even had my favorite – Lobster Newberg!

FOO YOO
Mine as well … Chicken Nuggets.

{they all stop and give FOO the evil eye – then continue with the task at hand}

NIGEL JAXX
I always feel a good meal is necessary before one conquers the world…
Easy my friends… easy! I do not want my greatest trophy to be damaged! There… yes!

{They place him in a rather unflattering pose and then all take a step back to admire their handiwork …}

BUSHYWOOD
Hmmm. He always seemed so much more --- I dunno – threatening when he was alive!

FOO YOO
Is true – perhaps this help…?

{*FOO moves up and positions BONDO in an odd position*}

NIGEL JAXX
No! NO! He was a lefty… the gun should be held like so …

{*JAXX moves up and positions BONDO in an odd position*}

BUSHYWOOD
Nah, that ain't right! He was definitely a righty, mate… and the gun was like this…

{*BUSHYWOOD moves up and positions BONDO in an odd position*}

ALEXIS
Hey! I got an idea – why don't we get some of these people to help – they seen him when he was alive… maybe they can pose him better than we can?

{*The others look about at the audience as though seeing them for the first time*}

FOO YOO
(*sotto voce to JAXX*)
How come you let people into lair?
(*motions to BONDO*)
He right… security suck.

NIGEL JAXX
Shut up! (*considering the idea for a beat*) Ms. Vulvae has an excellent suggestion … hmmm let me see…

{*JAXX selects two members of the audience to help and instructs them on how to best pose BONDO - this bit should play out pretty much like the improv game "Statues" – with audience members struggling to keep up with the bizarre suggestion thrown out by FOO, ALEXIS, JAXX and BUSHYWOOD – once the bit has gone on long enough, thank the audience members and then – back to the show!*}

NIGEL JAXX
Now then… the award ceremony…
With the use of this cute little space helmet, rigged with tiny nerve-gas capsules that were activated when the radio dials were twiddled (*whew, that's a mouthful!*) -- I am the one who has rid the world of the world's greatest super spy, James Bondo… I claim….

BUSHYWOOD
Not so fast, Jaxx.
You didn't kill Bondo --- I did!

NIGEL JAXX
What?

BUSHYWOOD
That's right... if all of you remember, before he put on your booby-trapped helmet, the creepy goofball in the fancy dress and I had maneuvered Bondo in between us when we had that little fracas earlier...

FOO YOO
Oh, yes... we chase around and round... he between us...
(*demonstrates in a humorous fashion*)

BUSHYWOOD
Well, when we was dancin' around him, I released a small puff of toxic dust from the poison ring I wear on my left hand (*she shows them all the ring, and how it flips open*)... this dust was concocted by an aboriginal witch-doctor friend of mine... distilled funnel-web spider venom, freeze dried then rendered into powder form... it's not exactly the fastest acting stuff on the planet, but it'll still kill ya deader than cat in a room full of pit bulls.

JAXX
Impossible!

ALEXIS
That's right... it is impossible. Because I'm the one who killed him!

FOO YOO
You crazy! Why you kill him when you all over him like horny toad at horndog convention … What? (*he points a finger at BUSHYWOOD*) She make stupid euphemism, I do too!

ALEXIS
Yeah, well, forget about that! I killed him when we locked lips!
You saw it, the way he dipped me… the passion, the fire!
Yeah, well he was dead right then… from my toxic lipstick!

BUSHYWOOD
Yer nuts, sister!
I poisoned him first!
The little dance me and Hong Kong Phooey did around Bondo took place before you kissed him!

ALEXIS
Yeah, but as you said… that powder of yours takes a while to get going, whereas the toxin in my lipstick went to work on his nervous system pretty much right away, burning him up with VX neurotoxin …
So my luscious lips trump your dumb ol' powder, sister!

NIGEL JAXX
Insanity!
He was killed by the nerve gas in my space helmet! Not from your archaic aboriginal powder trick or your idiotic and insufferable lip gloss!

BUSHYWOOD
Nice alliteration, pal!

FOO YOO
Please, allow me to burst all bubbles…
I am killer of Jason Bondo!

NIGEL JAXX
Impossible!

BUSHYWOOD
You're crazy!

ALEXIS
No way!

FOO YOO
Yes way!
(*he walks about, clicking his long fingernails together*)
Before he place booby-trapped helmet on head… before he swap spit with B-list actress… before he get face full of dried spider droppings… he get scratch on back of neck… from my fingernail coated with deadly Black Mamba venom!

NIGEL JAXX
Impossible!

BUSHYWOOD
You're crazy!

ALEXIS
No way!

{*FOO looks at all them as though they were crazy*}

FOO YOO
No repeats!
Is true… check body… you find scratch on neck… also have proof that my method is the one that kill him…

{JAXX, ALEXIS and BUSHYWOOD examine the body}

BUSHYWOOD
He's right… there's the scratch.

JAXX
But it does not prove anything!

ALEXIS
Yeah! Start talkin', creep!

FOO YOO
Funnel-web spider poison very deadly, but take hours to kill… the same is true of VX nerve toxin, take hours, not minutes… Honorable Jaxx not reveal name of his gas…

NIGEL JAXX
It is my own formula, I designed it myself… and it is a very fast acting agent, Foo.

FOO YOO
Oh, yeah!?

NIGEL JAXX
Yeah!

FOO YOO
Oh, yeah!??

NIGEL JAXX
YEAH!

FOO YOO
Well… shut up!

BUSHYWOOD
Nice. Look boys… we all can't claim to be the killer…

ALEXIS
She's right… only one of us killed him.
Trouble is… how do we know which one of us is the real killer?

NIGEL JAXX
The security tapes!
My facility is under constant video surveillance…

ALEXIS
Uh … I'm afraid not. I can't let anyone know I'm here… it could ruin my Hollywood rep… so I snuck into the security room and knocked out the guards there and set the video feeds on a loop…
(sheepish grin) Sorry!

FOO YOO
(*to JAXX*)
See! Security suck!

NIGEL JAXX

Well, we all can't have killed him... one of our methods must have done the job... the question is, which one?

{*they all stand around for a second, confused*}

FOO YOO

Ah... so.

(*he takes a beat, acknowledging the humorous connotation of that phrase*)

We come to crossroads, as they say... we all deliver deadly means to kill our enemy, but cannot say for certain which method was one that killed him.

BUSHYWOOD

Maybe we're missin' somethin' obvious . . . Let's ask the folks here if they have any questions which might help us clear up this mess. Okay, folks here's your chance to play secret agent... er, detective . . . we are gonna let ya ask each of us suspects a couple a questions about the gruesome death of Jason Bondo. First of all though, let's get this body off stage... (*JAXX and FOO help BONDO offstage*) Let's start the questioning with ALEXIS. (*pause*)
Are there any questions for NIGEL JAXX?
(*pause*)
How about FOO, any questions for him?
(*pause*)
And last but not least, myself, does anyone have any questions for me?
Okay folks, now that the questionin' is over with, it's time for you to solve this mystery. Find that sheet of paper inside your program marked Detective Sheet.
Now here's how to fill 'em out: . . . Write down the name of the person whom you think killed Double-O Zero.

Then write down why, and be as specific as possible, 'cause the one who comes closest to the right answers gonna win some mighty nice prizes, okay? After that, if y'all be so kind to flip the sheet over and fill out the little questionnaire on the back, we'd appreciate it.

If you want to know about upcoming shows we might be havin' be sure to include yer address and zip code and we'll add you to our mailin' list. That'll help us to keep bringing you more quality, educational programming like this fer years to come!

And most important of all, don't forget to sign yer name . . . you can't win a prize if we don't know the name of the person who won it!

We'll be back to collect those sheets in a moment.

END ACT TWO

ACT THREE

*MUSIC CUE

{the "evil lair theme" music of NIGEL JAXX announces the entrance of our cast of villains back for ACT III}

NIGEL JAXX
I tell you, it was the nerve gas from my carefully laid trap that killed him!

BUSHYWOOD
Forget it, Jaxx! Poison powder was his doom!

FOO YOO
Close pie hole! Or I scratch you with fingernail of venom!

ALEXIS
Give it a rest, all of ya! We're missin' the point!
(she pauses while the others look about in confusion)
Our number one nemesis is dead! No more foiled plots… we're free to take over the world!

NIGEL JAXX
Impossible!

BUSHYWOOD
You're crazy!

FOO
No way!

ALEXIS
Yes way!

***MUSIC CUE**
{*the KOOL & THE GANG song* **CELEBRATION** *fills the speakers and the villains all begin to dance about in, you guessed it, celebration – and then, suddenly it is cut off*}

NIGEL JAXX
Wait a minute – I'm here … Foo is here… Alexis… Ms. Bushywood…
(*he pulls a communicator out of his pocket and taps a few buttons*)
Then who is running the sound system?

BUSHYWOOD
Oh, no… that means…

ALEXIS
It can't be!

**MUSIC CUE – DRAMATIC STING

{*bounding in through the entrance comes the hero, JASON BONDO… back from the dead!
He wields his famous WPPK pistol, moving it back and forth between the villains*}

JASON BONDO
Hate to spoil the party folks, but I've got some world saving to do…

FOO YOO
Hey -- no fair! You dead!
We kill you!

JASON BONDO
Correction, Foo … you tried to kill me.
But I'm a secret agent…
I know villains such as you are always going to try and kill me…
so I have to be prepared.

BUSHYWOOD
But how…!?

JASON BONDO
How did I avoid being killed by the funnel-web powder you blew in my face?
Simple… I've got filters implanted in my nostrils … any poisonous or harmful substance I inhale is immediately filtered and destroyed.

FOO YOO
But how you escape venom scratch… it go right in your bloodstream!

JASON BONDO
A year ago, MI6 gave all of their agents a special transfusion – I've got synthetic blood Foo … blood that eats deadly snake venom for breakfast!

ALEXIS
My lipstick ploy was flawless! There's no way you could have…

JASON BONDO
Botox, sweetheart… my lips are completely fake and immune to poison.

NIGEL JAXX
(*moving backwards and revealing a gun*)
Very clever Double-O Zero – but then explain how you avoided inhaling the nerve toxin when you slipped the helmet on. I suppose you have fake lungs as well!

JASON BONDO
Don't be ridiculous, Jaxx… Fake lungs? What do you think this is? Science fiction?!

{*all of the characters start to laugh at the ludicrousness of this… but then stop and realize that they are performing an over-the-top murder mystery show*}

NIGEL JAXX
So explain your escape, Jason Bondo … how did you escape the nerve gas released by my booby-trapped space helmet.

JASON BONDO
Simple, Jaxx … though, you might want to get that explanation out of Ms. Bushywood…

BUSHYWOOD
(*she whips out her own gun and holds it on BONDO*)
Curse you Bondo – how much do you know?!

JASON BONDO
For starters, I know you're not really Shelia Bushywood... I eliminated the real Bushywood six months ago in Perth - you're really an ASIS operative... code name Mama Pajama!

{all of the others gasp in surprise}

BUSHYWOOD
That's right; the ASIS has gotten pretty tired of you hogging the spotlight, Bondo... so I took it upon myself to do you in. I disarmed the helmet when I was looking at it earlier!

NIGEL JAXX
You rotten no-good, double-agent, turncoat! The helmet was going to kill him... why disarm it!?

BUSHYWOOD
Better to be able to claim to be the actual killer than an accomplice...
I wanted the title belt, Jaxx ... now... hand it over... real slow like...

{just then, FOO drops his disguise, pulls off his hat and fake mustache, revealing his own pistol}

FOO YOO
(*still speaking in a bad oriental accent*)
Be as statue, Mama Pajama! The Chinese Special Branch will claim the title belt... as soon as I, Operative Purple Tiger kill all of you and report back to headquarters.

{just then, ALEXIS drops her disguise, revealing her own pistol}

ALEXIS
(*waves the pistol at all of them*)
Just take it easy there, Jackie Chan...
I think the CIA's gonna have something to say about that...

JASON BONDO
(*this is news to him*)
Wait a second, I knew Shelia was an Australian spy, I even knew Foo Yoo was a Chinese secret agent... but you are a secret agent too!?

ALEXIS
You bet your sweet bippy I am – Agent 69 – Code Name Kitty Diamond...
And with my very precious and very expensive diamond pistol, I'm gonna fill all of you with lead diamonds!

FOO YOO
How diamond be lead? That stupid!

ALEXIS
Shut up!
The CIA's been keeping tabs on all of you ... and now's the perfect time to take all of you out and make sure the CIA stays number 1 in the spy business.
Now... give me the title belt!

NIGEL JAXX
Enough of this stupidity!
(*he punches several buttons on his controller*)

***SFX CUE**

{*the sounds of gunshots is heard – a machine gun sound and BUSHYWOOD dies a gruesome death – a few sniper shots and FOO dies a gruesome death – several shotgun blasts and ALEXIS crumples to the floor, dead*}

JASON BONDO

Not bad, Jaxx… not bad at all… though you should've used a different caliber bullet … the Weatherby Magnum is pretty standard issue… for MI6!

NIGEL JAXX

(*dropping his fake East German accent and adopting a clipped British one*)

Oooooh, I really hate you! It's about time a new secret agent took your place and that secret agent is me – Agent Double-O Eighty-Five!
Who's got the game all figured out now, huh Mr. Goody Two Shoes?
Mr. I'm-so-cool, Agent Double-O Zero!

{*BONDO does a really silly distraction maneuver – something along the lines of doing a silly rope-a-dope with his feet and tossing his gun back and forth between his hands really quickly before firing off a shot at JAXX that knocks the villain's gun out of his hand*}

JASON BONDO

I guess that's the way the cookie crumbles, Agent 85.
Now, are you gonna come quietly or…

NIGEL JAXX

The belt is mine! I won it fair and square … by cheating!
You can't have it!

{*he tries to put the belt on but BONDO shoots him, he dies in a hilarious and overly dramatic way – BONDO looks about the room at the mess*}

JASON BONDO

Well, I guess that about wraps it up… better check in with M…

{*he walks over to JAXX, picks up the helmet and puts on, twiddles the dials and begins speaking…*}

JASON BONDO

Headquarters? This is Bondo, Jason Bondo… I just *cough* - *CHOKE*!!!

{*BONDO struggles with the nerve gas but succumbs, dropping to the floor dead! … and then over the speaker system we hear an evil laugh…. Muhaha … Muhaha! MUHAHAHA!*}

THE END

DEATH COMES TO GOTHAMVILLE

Or

"WHO BUMPED OFF OMEGA, MAN?!"

By
David J. Fielding
Copyright © 2011

SETTING

All of the action of this Super Heroic Comedy-Mystery takes place in the Hall of Freedom, the headquarters of the Justice Force, a crime-fighting organization of super-powered heroes; located in downtown Pittsburgh.
All the actors mingle in with the audience before the show begins, dropping hints, suggestions and innuendo about their pasts.

CHARACTERS

OMEGAMAN – Born on the distant world of Krapton, this super-being adopted our world as his own and vowed to use his powers to rid the earth of the criminal elements that were running rampant throughout the towns and cities of the world. For the last thirty years, OMEGAMAN has been a beacon of hope, truth and justice for the common people.
OMEGAMAN is a Superman™ pastiche.

******

WONDRA – Raised on a remote island by a society of Feminist Greenpeace Revolutionaries, WONDRA is the ultimate warrior. She uses her fantastic strength, beauty and fighting skills to battle the forces of evil where ever they threaten the free world… especially the coffee bean fields of South America, because, well… she needs her coffee dammit!

WONDRA is a Wonder Woman™ pastiche.

******

THE COWL – Billionaire industrialist by day, indomitable crime-fighting avenger by night, THE COWL roots out evil wherever it may hide. Outfitting himself with gadgets and high-tech crime-deterrent equipment, THE COWL is ready for any and every situation… he even keeps a spare tux on hand, just in case a supermodel or movie starlet needs and emergency escort.
THE COWL is a Batman™ pastiche.

******

RAPIDO – When he was blasted into a vat of radioactive material by a bolt of electricity from a faulty fuse box, Barney Allmen was transformed into the fastest creature on the planet. Able to move at speeds faster than the blink of an eye, RAPIDO took to stopping crime before it can even begin.
RAPIDO is a Flash™ pastiche.

******

JINX - Born into a family of mystical royalty, JINX is a true magician. Using her magical powers to combat the criminal element all across the globe, the Mistress of Mystery fears nothing and no on. She also is a world-famous fashion designer and is always dressed to kill… just look at those thigh-highs! Roawrr!
JINX is a Zatanna™ pastiche.

******

BEACON – Granted his powers through the use of an alien power source contained in his ring, BEACON is the foe of any criminal who hides in the shadows or who operates under the cover of darkness. During the day he's pretty darn useless… but at night, watch out!

BEACON is a Green Lantern™ pastiche.

(**NOTE:** *BEACON is played by the same actor who plays OMEGAMAN*)

AUDIENCE PARTICIPATION CHARACTERS

The following characters are 'one-liners', audience members selected during the mingle and who are handed their lines before the show begins. All of the Audience Participation Characters in this show are members of Mongoose's entourage.

Timmy Ohlman – cub reporter for PNN – Planet News Network
Valerie Vickers – independent news photographer and investigative reporter
Lara Lansing – anchor woman, PNN – Planet News Network

FUN FACTS

The following facts should be printed out and placed on the tables around the room – one fact per table and spread out.
Tables are encouraged to exchange information they receive on each Fun Fact.

OMEGAMAN – The most powerful human on Earth, OMEGAMAN is a name known all around the globe. He is the epitome of truth, justice and looking good no matter what the occasion – be it a knock-down drag out in a construction zone to a red carpet premiere – hey, he's OMEGAMAN!

WONDRA – A member of Amazonian royalty, WONDRA is also OMEGAMAN's off again/on again romantic interest. Their relationship has been a rocky one – lots of skirmishes which end up in kind of embarrassing make-out sessions with the whole world watching.

THE COWL – A dark hero who operates from the shadows, he's always been second choice when the world is looking for someone to save them from an alien invasion or an attack from giant robots. THE COWL would do just about anything to gain the level of respect that OMEGAMAN has… anything.

BEACON – A member of a Galactic Force of Crime Fighter's BEACON has been butting heads with OMEGAMAN for years about who is the most powerful hero of them all. Each year they compete on the Battle of the Network Superstars, with the shows generally ending in a tie – that is until last year's show when OMEGAMAN won by 5 points!

RAPIDO – Several months ago, RAPIDO was involved in an industrial waste accident and temporarily lost his superspeed powers. He was pretty upset about being called the Far From the Fastest Human alive.

JINX – Her father, The Great Zoltan, was one of the first super villains and an enemy of OMEGAMAN. Though her father ended up in an insane asylum, JINX has vowed to make up for her father's evil ways by using her powers strictly for good – well, most of the time anyway.

PRODUCTION NOTES

The following notes are given to give the cast ideas and suggestions for setting and production.

COSTUMES – Costumes should be as complete as possible and should give the audience information and clues about each of the characters.

- **OMEGAMAN** – should be dressed in blue and white with a blue cape. The cast is encouraged to get together and come up with symbols or logos for each of the heroes.

- **WONDRA** – should be dressed as like an Amazonian Warrior Princess – more Xena than Wonder Woman. The cast is encouraged to get together and come up with symbols or logos for each of the heroes.

- **THE COWL**– should be dressed fairly close to the Dark Knight himself, all grays and blacks, spooky black cape. His full head mask should have ears, but they should be different that a bat's… more cat-like perhaps. The cast is encouraged to get together and come up with symbols or logos for each of the heroes.

- **BEACON** – should be dressed in reds and greens, with a black domino mask and green cape. The cast is encouraged to get together and come up with symbols or logos for each of the heroes.

- **JINX** – should be dressed ala a female stage magician – tux coat, fishnets and top hat – thigh-high boots. The cast is encouraged to get together and come up with symbols or logos for each of the heroes.

• **RAPIDO** – should be dressed all in orange with purple accents; his pants should have a number of cargo pockets to hide the props used for visual gags. The cast is encouraged to get together and come up with symbols or logos for each of the heroes.

A NOTE ON THE PLAYING SPACE – There are a number of stage props that need to have a fixed position in the show – these include the Hall of Freedom's Supercomputer, the Crisis BEACON and the Freedom Screen. These items can be as elaborate or simple or as cheesy as the cast sees fit.
Supercomputer – This prop can be as small as a toaster oven or as larger as the space/transporting of the item will allow – the cast is encouraged to familiarize themselves with it, so anyone of them knows which buttons do what.

Crisis Beacon – The Crisis Beacon is probably best represented by a flashing police-light or something similar; it can also be part of the Supercomputer, if need be.
Freedom Screen – The large viewing screen the heroes use to access views of crisis spots around the globe – it can be super fancy (*flat screen TV*) or kinda cheap (*tin foil in a picture frame*).

A NOTE ON CHARACTER GENDER – Though the script has been written with each of the characters being acted by a certain sex, there is absolutely no reason why parts cannot be switched or exchanged. WONDRA is probably the only role that should stay as written – to be played by a female – but all of the others can be played by either sex with minor changes to the text.

A NOTE ON THE SFX and MUSIC – There are a number of SFX cues in the show and the author has tried to arrange it so that at least one cast member is off stage in order to cue them up and play them over the sound system. Music for the show should be comprised of both popular music and cinematic soundtracks from 'heroic' action movies. See below for suggestions.

{*During the actor's mingle some appropriate music should play over the sound system – following is a suggested list of songs with a 'superhero' theme:*
"Jimmy Olsen's Blues," Spin Doctors;
"Kryptonite," 3 Doors Down;
"Superman," R.E.M.;
"Party Man," Prince;
"Weird Science," Oingo Boingo;
"Flash (Theme from Flash Gordon)," Queen;
"Believe it or Not (The Greatest American Hero)," Joey Scarbury, etc.
Suggestions for "heroic" action movie music that can be used between the songs are:
"The Avengers," Alan Silvestri – Marvel's The Avengers;
"Driving with the Top Down," Ramin Dwadji – Iron Man;
"Vespertilio," Hans Zimmer and James Newton Howard – Batman Begins;
"Saving the World," John Ottman – Superman Returns;
"X-Training," Henry Jackman – X-Men: First Class;
"Main Title," Craig Armstrong – The Incredible Hulk;
"Overture," Jerry Goldsmith – Supergirl, etc.}

ACT ONE

{After the mingle, and once the Audience Participation Characters have been selected, the music should fade and then the lights will dim.
As the house lights fade, the SFX/Music Track 1 should play: This track should begin with a stirring "superhero-esque" piece of music – either John William's "Superman Theme (Main Title March)" or something similar – this should segue into the SFX of a terrific battle with sounds of crashes, metal twisting, etc punctuated with terrific explosions.
The lights should come up to reveal LUCY LANNISTER (**Note** LUCY LANNISTER is played by the same actress who plays WONDRA) standing in the front of the playing space, microphone in hand and speaking as though she were reporting "on the scene"...}

***SFX/MUSIC CUE**

LUCY LANNISTER

This is LUCY LANNISTER, Planet News Network, reporting from the center of Gothamville where a massive battle is underway between the Justice Force and Rex Ruthless and his legion of robot drones! The so called Master of Disaster is holding the city hostage, threatening nuclear destruction and has been confronted by OMEGAMAN and the rest of the Justice Force…. If they cannot defeat this evil plot, then that madman will see Gothamville destroyed!

***SFX/MUSIC CUE**

{the SFX of a rush of powerful wind is heard and OMEGAMAN (**Note** OMEGAMAN is played by the same actor who plays

BEACON) leaps in through the entrance, cape billowing and a broad winning, confident smile on his face –
Enter OMEGAMAN}

OMEGAMAN
(*waving to the audience*)
Have no fear, Omegaman is here!

LUCY LANNISTER
(*smitten*)
Oh! Omegaman!
You're here to save me… uh; I mean us… I mean the city!

OMEGAMAN
(*smiling and winking*)
Yes. Yes I am!
Stand back now…

{another SFX of wind is heard and OMEGAMAN leaps back through the entrance, leaving LUCY LANNISTER to describe the ensuing battle –
Exit OMEGAMAN}

LUCY LANNISTER
Ladies and gentlemen, the Justice Force is battling for our very lives! No matter the outcome, I and PNN will be here to bring all the details of this terrific battle to save the city!

***SFX/MUSIC CUE**

{SFX representing an object moving at very high speed is heard and RAPIDO runs in through the entrance, screeching to a halt and striking a heroic pose –
Enter RAPIDO}

RAPIDO
(*looking LUCY up and down*)
Hey, hey there Lucy!

LUCY LANNISTER
(*taken aback*)
RAPIDO!
What are you doing!? Shouldn't you be helping defeat the robot drones?!

RAPIDO
(*leaning up against a wall, unconcerned*)
Oh, I am…
(*he makes a quick move to the LEFT - the gag here is that he is so fast he leaves and is back before anyone can see him move*)
Just took out three of 'em on the roof over on 34th and Lake…
(*he makes a quick move to the RIGHT – same gag, different direction*)
…and three more that were setting up a laser turret down the street.

LUCY LANNISTER
(*confused*)
But… but you didn't even leave the room?!

RAPIDO
(*he gives her a sly wink*)
You sure about that…?
Fastest man alive, honey! Oh and speaking of honey… I saw your boyfriend OMEGAMAN whispering in JINX's ear not too long ago… Uh-oh… more of Rex's drones are threatening the energy plant across town! Gotta dash!

***SFX/MUSIC CUE**

{*another SFX of whining speed is heard as RAPIDO runs back through the entrance, leaving LUCY LANNISTER behind –*
Exit RAPIDO}

LUCY LANNISTER
(*shouting after RAPIDO*)
He was chatting up that spell-weaving hussy? Why I oughta….! (*catching herself*) Oh, uh… Ladies and gentlemen the battle continues to rage as … Look out!!
*SFX/MUSIC CUE

{*SFX of a massive crash, the sound of twisting metal and exploding concrete is followed by some magical spell or zapping sounds and JINX runs in through the entrance, making mystical waving signs with her hands –*
Enter JINX}

JINX
(*glancing over her shoulder at LUCY*)
Better get under cover Miss Lannister!
(*glaring up at something overhead*)
BEACON …BEACON!
Stop showboating and take those flying dumbots out of the air!
*SFX/MUSIC CUE

{*SFX of bolt of mystical energy sounds and then we hear BEACON's voice - LUCY and JINX look up, telling us that BEACON is somewhere overhead –*
V.O. BEACON}

BEACON (V.O.)
(*annoyed*)
Don't get your fishnets in a twist sweetheart! I got it covered!

JINX
(*miffed*)
Stop worrying about everyone's panties and get the job done, you big oaf!
(*to LUCY*) Men! … Speaking of which, I got some ugly butts to kick… outta my way!

***SFX/MUSIC CUE**

{*SFX of mystical energies being cast and JINX exits the stage. LUCY continues to describe the scene –*
Exit JINX}

LUCY LANNISTER
(*continues to report on the battle*)
The Justice Force certainly seems to have their hands full! Rex Ruthless has pulled out all the stops and is throwing everything he can at our heroes!

***SFX/MUSIC CUE**

{*SFX of some brutal punches and kicks and then THE COWL leaps onto the stage, in one hand he has what looks to be a smart phone. THE COWL barks orders into the phone, looking about the battlefield –*
Enter THE COWL}

THE COWL
(*gruffly*)
RAPIDO, rendezvous with BEACON at Central Plaza; JINX, cover sectors 9, 12 and 15…
OMEGAMAN! I've pinpointed Rex's location…
I need you to be at these exact coordinates in order to take him out!
(*he's looking directly at LUCY*)

Where's WONDRA!?!

LUCY LANNISTER
(*doing a poor job of covering*)
Uh, I … uh… saw her… over there… yeah… by the PNN Building!

THE COWL
(*suspicious*)
You look… familiar…

LUCY LANISTER
(*turning away*)
Yeah… well, I am on TV you know!
(*gasps*)
Look out! The PNN Globe's about to fall!
***SFX/MUSIC CUE**

{*SFX of squealing metal and breaking glass, as THE COWL rushes offstage… and then we hear the SFX of rushing wind as LUCY LANNISTER describes the scene –*
Eixt THE COWL}

LUCY LANNISTER
OH MY! This is terrible! The famous PNN Globe atop PNN Tower has been blasted off its base and is rolling toward the edge of the building! If it falls it will crush the throng of people below! Somebody do something!
***SFX/MUSIC CUE**

{*SFX of crashing sounds and then rushing wind*}

LUCY LANNISTER
This is amazing!
OMEGAMAN has stopped the globe from falling!
Let's hear it for OMEGAMAN!

***SFX/MUSIC CUE**

{*the SFX of a rush of powerful wind is heard and OMEGAMAN leaps in through the entrance once more, that same smug smile on his face –* Enter OMEGAMAN}

OMEGAMAN
(*waving to the audience*)
Have no fear, OMEGAMAN is here - again!

LUCY LANNISTER
(*smitten*)
Congratulations OMEGAMAN! You've saved the city once again!

OMEGAMAN
(*smiling and winking*)
Yes. Yes I did!

LUCY LANNISTER
(*trying to remain composed*)
Tell us, OMEGAMAN… how is it you were able to defeat the most ruthless and evil villain of all time once again?

OMEGAMAN
(*striking a heroic pose*)
Well, Lucy… it was a tough and grueling battle, but in the end, Rex made the one mistake all villains make…

LUCY LANNISTER
(*turning back to the audience*)
Well, all of us are certainly grateful for all of your efforts!

OMEGAMAN
(*smiling and winking*)
Well, Lucy… it's certainly a pleasure to…
(*OMEGAMAN suddenly begins to choke, grasping at his throat, clawing for breath*)
URK! GASP! *gurgle* Argh!

LUCY LANNISTER
(*horrified*)
OMEGAMAN! Oh! What's happening?!

OMEGAMAN
(*dies in an over the top manner, falling back through the entrance*)
Arrrgh!

{*Exit OMEGAMAN*}

LUCY LANNISTER
(*distraught*)
Oh no! No! OMEGAMAN's dead! The world's most powerful superhero has been murdered!

{*we hear a dramatic burst of music and the lights dim as we transition to the Hall of Freedom, headquarters of the Freedom Force – we hear the transition cue (ala the same type of cue used in the cartoon Super Friends)*
Exit LUCY LANNISTER}

{After the next short bit of dialogue, enter into the playing space THE COWL, RAPIDO and JINX, each one striking a dramatic pose, each one on cue with the accompanying V.O. :}

***SFX/MUSIC CUE**

V.O. (*on tape*)
Meanwhile back at the Hall of Freedom...
Though the battle with Rex Ruthless is won, a pall of gloom fills the heroes headquarters with a terrible chill - the news of OMEGAMAN's death has hit our heroes hard, knocking the wind out of the sails of our otherwise stalwart band of protectors...

RAPIDO, the fastest human on the planet...

{Enter RAPIDO}

JINX, Mistress of Magic and Mayhem...

{Enter JINX}

And THE COWL, dark protector of Gothamville...

{Enter THE COWL}

Three founding members of the Justice Force gather to mourn and to ask the burning question...
Who killed OMEGAMAN!?

RAPIDO
(*smacking one fist into his hand*)
OMEGAMAN's been murdered! Holy Unexpected Event!

JINX
(*crossing further into the room*)
It's unbelievable! He was impervious!
Bullets, bombs, high-powered lasers… deodorant!
Nothing pierced his skin!

THE COWL
(*brooding darkly*)
It seems that the indestructible man was destructible after all…

RAPIDO
(*narrows his eyes*)
That's pretty cold, Cowl…

THE COWL
(*glaring darkly at RAPIDO*)
Death is cold… Death is a dark mistress, unforgiving, cruel and final…
One cannot court Death and remain… alive.

JINX
(*smirking*)
Thanks for putting that in perspective Captain Downer…

THE COWL
(*not really comprehending*)
I'm THE COWL…
Captain Downer is just a silly comic book character…

JINX
(*rolling her eyes*)

Whatever! Look, we need to figure out what happened... where are the others?

RAPIDO

(*smacking his fist into his hand*)
JINX is right! Where's BEACON? Where's WONDRA?

THE COWL

(*striding over to a designated area of the playing space and accessing the SUPERCOMPUTER*)
I'll pinpoint their locations using the GPS triangulation system and then contact them via satellite uplink...

JINX

(*whips out her smart phone, exasperated*)
Or! We could just text them...

RAPIDO

(*getting their attention*)
Uh, guys... Fastest being on the planet...
I could just run and find out...

JINX

(*eyes widening*)
OK, so... go! Find them!

RAPIDO

Right!
(*he makes a motion as though he is about to run off to the LEFT – repeating the gag from the top of the show*)
Ok, BEACON's on his way, he just got through his second shift at Chippendale's...

(*he makes a motion as though he is about to run off to the RIGHT – same gag as before but this time he rubs his face as though he has been smacked*)
WONDRA… well, uh she was… indisposed… OW.
***SFX/MUSIC CUE**

{*Enter WONDRA to a burst of dramatic music -*

And boy is she pissed! She's steaming mad, carrying a towel and charges after RAPIDO who hop skips and jumps to keep out of her reach}

WONDRA

(*fists clenched, storming after RAPIDO*)
C'mere ya good for nothing peeping tom!
Can't a gal shower in peace in this town!?

RAPIDO

(*yelping*)
Hey! We just needed to know if you were on your way to the Hall of Freedom!
The big guy's been murdered for cryin' out loud!

THE COWL

(*stepping between the two bickering heroes*)
Alright you two… cut it out.
We have a serious situation which is going to require us to pull together as a team!
We don't have time for bickering and petty indiscretions…

WONDRA

(*rounding on COWL*)

Petty indiscretions?! It's a matter of privacy you leather clad weirdo!

JINX
(*taking the chance to get a dig in on WONDRA*)
Please…! Like you haven't had every other man in this city up to your (makes finger quotes) penthouse.

RAPIDO
(*stifling a giggle*)
Oh, snap!

WONDRA
(*stepping menacingly toward JINX*)
You gotta a lotta nerve… oh wait -- I forgot. There's that whole issue of you having never been kissed… What's a matter, sister? Jealous?

THE COWL
(*face palm*)
How on earth do we ever manage to thwart evil…? Trying to lead this team is like herding cats.

RAPIDO
(*doesn't like the sound of that*)
Hold the phone! Who made you leader!?!

WONDRA
(*snarling at RAPIDO*)
Justice Force by laws … Cowl here is de facto leader in the event of OMEGAMAN's disappearance, demise or his bi-annual two week vacation in Tierra del Fuego. Don't you ever read the newsletter?

RAPIDO
(*tries to stand up to her and fails*)
Yeah, well… shut up!
I tried to read the newsletter…. But JINX used 'em all to line the kitty box of that magical cat of hers!

JINX
(*starts to retort, but regains her composure*)
You know what…!
Never mind… I hate to admit it, but Cowl's right.
We need to work together!

THE COWL
(*throwing his shoulders back*)
And that's just what we are going to do… as soon as Bacon gets here.

RAPIDO
(*confused*)
Who?

THE COWL
(*throwing his shoulders back*)
Bacon.

RAPIDO
(*still confused*)
Sorry… doesn't ring a bell…

WONDRA
(*smacking RAPIDO upside the head*)
BEACON ya moron…!
He means BEACON.

THE COWL
(*covering*)
Right… like I said… Bacon.
Beaker.
BEACON.

JINX
(*hands on her hips*)
Hoo-boy… how quickly things fall apart when the second stringer gets a shot at command.

RAPIDO
(*confused*)
We have a second in command?

WONDRA
(*glaring at RAPIDO*)
Take a seat, Speedy…
All that zipping around has dislodged what little brains you got in that tiny head of yours.
Ok Mr. Dark and Mysterious… so what's our first move?

THE COWL
(*he looks about*)
I've taken the liberty of uploading the news footage of OMEGAMAN's last exchange with LUCY LANNISTER … you should be able to watch it on your wrist communicator devices.

JINX
(*trying not to sound impressed*)
Wow… we can?
I mean, how the heck did you arrange that?
We all got to the Hall of Freedom at the same time… I haven't
seen you messing with any of the computers or nothing…!

THE COWL
(*ominously*)
I have my secrets.

RAPIDO
(*excited*)
Cool! I love it when we get to play with all the neat high-tech
gadgets!

***SFX/MUSIC CUE**

{*Enter BEACON to a burst of dramatic music - He enters waving,
shaking hands, high-fiving the audience. BEACON is "the ladies' man"-
swaggering, full of himself and striking poses, showing off his pecs and
inviting females "to the gun show"*}

BEACON
(*after his entrance, finally acknowledging the others*)
Hidey-ho, everybody!
Wow, did we do something different to the Freedom Hall… 'cause
it sure looks AWESOME!

RAPIDO
(*looking about*)
Uh, no… looks pretty much the same as it always has…

WONDRA
(*smacking RAPIDO upside the head*)
He's being a jerk, jerk! (*to BEACON*) Listen up Lite-Brite… we've been waiting on you to get things underway… you do know OMEGAMAN's been murdered right?

BEACON
(*with a wry grin*)
Yeah, yeah… I caught Cowl's transmission on my wrist communicator.
Hard to believe that the big O has gone bye-bye…

WONDRA
(*snidely, to JINX*)
Too bad some of us never even got to experience even a little O…

JINX
(*daggers in her eyes*)
Better no O than a big Ho!

RAPIDO
(*sotto voce to COWL*)
Fifty Bucks WONDRA wipes the floor with JINX…

THE COWL
(*acts disgusted… and then hands some cash to RAPIDO*)
I'll take those odds…

RAPIDO
(*sniggering*)
Heh! Easy money!

{*at this point the CRISIS BEACON suddenly sounds and flashes alerting the JUSTICE FORCE – and the AUDIENCE – that an emergency situation is at hand! This bit is optional and in no way has a bearing on the plot – and is simply included as a fun/funny bit for the audiences' amusement. The CAST is encouraged to change these up for each performance – as a way to keep the script fresh, to add their own flavor to the show or to play pranks on other actors – the bits included here are scripted and can be used, but are by no means set in stone...*}

***SFX/MUSIC CUE**

{*The CRISIS BEACON flares to life - After three blaring tones are heard the SFX will end ... the BEACON's LIGHT will continue to flash until shut off by one of the characters who reaches the SUPERCOMPUTER to throw the switch that shuts it off **If budget or tech constraints will not allow the BEACON – it is recommended that these bits be cut from the show ** THE COWL presses a button on the SUPERCOMPUTER which plays the V.O. that accompanies this gag/bit... the V.O. should be able to be played from on stage via an MP3 or CD set up that is part of the SUPERCOMPTER*}

THE COWL

(*leaping into action, and pressing the button to activate the V.O.*)
This is the Justice Force Crisis Hotline! What is your emergency!

V.O. (*on tape*)

(*CELEBRITY VOICE impersonated*)
Justice Force – This is the President!
There is an emergency that requires your immediate attention!

WONDRA

(*eager*)
What is it, Mr. President?!

V.O. (*on tape*)
Well, this isn't one of your typical giant robot emergencies or even an alien invasion... but it's still damn important – I'm missing my jar of jelly beans!

JINX
(*dumbfounded*)
Uh – your what!?

V.O. (*on tape*)
Jelly Beans, Missy! Jelly Beans!
A man needs his jelly beans if he's gonna size up the leaders of other nations!
Look, how's a man supposed to tell if them Ruskies are bluffin' or if they're ready to push the button!?
See, if they choose the white jelly beans... they're all friendly like... they choose red and KABOOM!

THE COWL
(*perturbed*)
We'll have to get back to Mr. President... we are... about to engage in a battle with some... uh... bad guys...

V.O. (*on tape*)
Fine! But you get back to as soon as you can! I need them jelly beans!

{*In disgust, THE COWL snaps off the V.O. The heroes all look at each other for a beat.*}

WONDRA
(*hands up*)
Don't look at me ... I didn't vote for him!

RAPIDO
(*bright*)
I could go for some jelly beans actually… I hear the green ones increase the time you can…

JINX
(*points a finger at him*)
Finish that sentence and I will flash-fry your underwear…

BEACON
(*back to business*)
Well we certainly have a pretty ugly mess on our hands with OMEGAMAN's murder. The people of Gothamville adored OMEGAMAN… they're gonna want his killer's head on a plate.
(*walks about, acting nonchalant*)
So, which one of you was the one who got ballsy enough to do the deed, huh?

JINX
(*startled*)
What!? Whoa, whoa, whoa…
Are you actually accusing one of us of murdering OMEGAMAN?

RAPIDO
(*getting it*)
Hey! Didn't none of us kill him! We're the good guys!

THE COWL
(*taking out a *device* and punching buttons*)
I had reached the same conclusion, Bacon…

BEACON
(*annoyed*)
The name's BEACON, bat-brain...

THE COWL
(*continuing to futz with his *device**)
Right, that's what I said... Bacon...
Beaker. BEACON.
But the fact remains, ten seconds after the news cameras caught OMEGAMAN's last gasps, I deduced that OMEGAMAN's death was caused by a none other than a member of the Justice Force...
One of us in this room... is a killer.

WONDRA
(*hands on her hips*)
Seriously? That's insane... Speedfreak is right, we are the good guys – we're not killers – heck all of the villains we fight we haul off to jail...
Ain't none of us here ever put anyone six feet under!

JINX
(*with conviction*)
Yeah! And besides... none of us was anywhere near OMEGAMAN when he collapsed!

RAPIDO
(*agreeing*)
She's right! Why accuse us... why can't it be one of the bad guys? Rex Ruthless, or Medulla-12, or Chilly Willy!?

THE COWL
(*holding his *device* and entering info into the SUPERCOMPUTER*)
Chilly Willy is a cartoon Penguin, my hyperactive homey...

BEACON
(*annoyed*)
Did you just actually use the word homey?

THE COWL
(*continues entering info into the SUPERCOMPUTER*)
Alliteration is sometimes necessary in order to bring to light that which we sometimes forget…
Though we all stand accused, we are all still teammates.
All of you; are my homeys.

JINX
(*creeped out*)
I really don't think I want to be your homey, Cowl…

THE COWL
(*finishing with the SUPERCOMPUTER and turning to the others*)
No matter, I have already classified you all as my homeys on my Facebook page…

WONDRA
(*incredulous*)
You!? Have a Facebook page!?
Isn't that … like against the superhero code or something?

THE COWL
(*finishing with the SUPERCOMPUTER and turning to the others*)
It's not only a social and networking tool; it's actually a good way to keep tabs on bad guys…
You would be surprised at how many criminals brag of their exploits in their status updates…

But to answer your question, RAPIDO, at this moment in time, all of our major nemeses are either locked up tight in the Gothamville City Jail or Stillwater Sanitarium.
There are no more bad guys... we are the only suspects.

RAPIDO
(*dismayed*)
Well... that... sucks!

BEACON
(*arms crossed*)
I hate to burst your bubble, JINX...
But you are wrong about us not being near OMEGAMAN before he died...

THE COWL
(*entering info into the SUPERCOMPUTER*)
I've analyzed the video feed of the PNN broadcast of the battle with Rex Ruthless...
Each of us is, at one point or another, very close to OMEGAMAN... any of us could've used that time to murder him.

JINX
(*startled*)
Wait a minute!? How the heck is that possible?
OMEGAMAN died after the battle was over... and after he was well away from any of us...
How the heck do you explain that?

RAPIDO
(*siding with her*)
Yeah! How the heck do you explain that?!

THE COWL
(still making calculations on the SUPERCOMPUTER)
As all of us are intimately aware, OMEGAMAN had only one weakness…

BEACON
(sagely)
Kraptonite.

WONDRA
(startled)
Yeah. Kraptonite… we all knew that…
Heck everybody in the world knows that…!

RAPIDO
(siding with her)
Yeah!
Everybody knows that!

WONDRA
(grabbing RAPIDO by the collar)
Zip it, pal… how's about instead of just agreeing with me and JINX, you add something original to the mix!?!

RAPIDO
(uncomprehending)
What… like rice? I'm not real good in the kitchen…

THE COWL
(finishes his calculations and turns to face the others)
Kraptonite is… or should I say - was… OMEGAMAN's only true weakness.

Even the smallest amount could weaken him, rendering him powerless...

BEACON
(*picking up*)
Or, kill him. One of us managed to expose OMEGAMAN to this deadly substance... which affected him after he had moved away from whoever exposed him to it... it's the only way to explain his death. All we need to do is to determine how it was administered to him...

JINX
(*wary*)
You guys seem to have this all figured out.

THE COWL
(*adjusting his gloves, proudly*)
Well, I am the world's greatest criminologist...

BEACON
(*sagely*)
And I'm attuned to the cosmic vibrations of the universe...

RAPIDO
(*brightening*)
Hey! I vibrate all the time too!

JINX
(*repulsed*)
That is disgusting!

WONDRA
(*suspicious*)
I find it pretty weird that you two are suddenly all buddy-buddy and in agreement!
We all know you two are usually at each other's throats and only OMEGAMAN's leadership kept you two from having a sissy man slap fight... what gives?

JINX
(*siding with WONDRA*)
Yeah! WONDRA's got a point!
Maybe you two cooked up this little scheme to frame one of us and make it look like neither of you had anything to do with it ... when in reality it was a two man job, am I right!?

RAPIDO
(*confused*)
Wait... COWL and BEACON are... together? Like... boyfriends?
(*hands up*)
Not that I have a problem with that... good for you guys!!

BEACON
(*steps away from COWL*)
Now hold on a minute!

THE COWL
(*with a dramatic sweep of his cape as he steps after*)
There's no use denying it, Bacon... why should we hide our feelings any longer...
They were bound to find out sooner or later!

BEACON
(*keeps moving away from COWL*)

Ah… heh… OK, fun's over!
(he runs and stands next to the AUDIENCE MEMBER picked to read LARA LANSING)
I, uh… I got a girlfriend! Isn't that right, sweetheart!

LARA LANSING
Uh, I guess? I mean… we were supposed to go out last week… But you backed out at the last minute.

BEACON
(getting closer)
Hey, there was a galactic crisis - I had to stop the Shia-LaBeouf Empire from invading!

LARA LANSING
He's an actor, not an Empire… listen, jerk. Why not try telling a girl the truth, huh?

BEACON
(getting closer)
I told you… saving the world, that's kinda my thing!

LARA LANSING
Saving the world? Yeah… like you could do that by yourself!

BEACON
That's it! We are so broken up!

LARA LANSING
Fine by me… I think THE COWL is cuter anyway!!

BEACON
Shows you how much you know!
(*pointing to COWL*)
I happen to know for a fact that he's already got a girlfriend!

JINX
(*really surprised*)
He does?!

WONDRA
(*smirking*)
Oh, this I gotta hear about… Mr. Creep-in-the-Shadows has got a girl?

BEACON
Yep! She's even been to his secret cave hideout!
(he runs and stands next to the AUDIENCE MEMBER picked to read LARA LANSING)
Isn't that right, Ms. Vickers!

VALERIE VICKERS
That's right.
He even drove me there in that beat up Honda Civic of his.

THE COWL
(*turns his back on her*)
It's not a Honda! It's THE COWL CAR!
It's a special design I created… it's got armor plating, machine guns… a fully stocked mini-bar and an MP3 player!

VALERIE VICKERS
Sure, sure… Oh and the cave? It had this really weird smell…

WONDRA
What?
Like old socks and man-sweat?

VALERIE VICKERS
Actually it was kinda sweet smelling… like strawberries and Chanel No. 5.

THE COWL
(*spins and points a finger*)
It's aromatherapy for meditation purposes! It helps me think!

VALERIE VICKERS
Which is all that happens in the Cowl Cave… a real let down if you ask me.

RAPIDO
(*confused*)
Wait a minute…
I thought you guys said that COWL and BEACON were… so how come they got's girlfriends?
(*rubs his temples*)
I'm really confused!!

JINX
(*trying to rein things in*)
Ok, look … we are getting off track here…
The main thing is to focus on OMEGAMAN's murder ok? Not who's schtupping who…

WONDRA
(*grudgingly*)
You're right… so what do we know so far?
OMEGAMAN was most likely killed by Kraptonite exposure…
which of you jerks had access to Kraptonite?

BEACON
(*accusing COWL*)
What about you, Mister!
Who knows what the heck you've been up to in that cave of yours?
And you've got a secret stash of Kraptonite, don't 'cha?

THE COWL
(*rubbing his jaw thoughtfully*)
I must admit, I did have a chunk of Kraptonite in my vault.
I was studying its properties in order to see if I could find a way to develop an antidote for OMEGAMAN…

RAPIDO
(*proud of himself*)
A-ha! Cowl plus Kraptonie equals a dead OMEGAMAN!

JINX
(*scowling*)
Can it, ding dong. Cowl's had that piece of Kraptonite for years … we all knew about it.
It doesn't prove he's the killer… it just makes him more of a suspect.
That piece of Kraptonite still in your vault, Cowl?

THE COWL
(*hates to admit it*)
Unfortunately, no.

It was stolen last week.

WONDRA
(*gloating*)
Ha! That's rich! The world's greatest criminologist got his house robbed!

BEACON
(*also taking the chance to stick it to COWL*)
A week ago!? Why didn't you tell any of us?
Afraid we might laugh at you?

{*The cast takes a beat and then they all laugh at COWL*}

THE COWL
(*trying to remain calm but not doing a good job*)
Stop it! Criminology takes time…
Not all of us have cosmic powers or magic to aid us in our battle against the forces of evil!

RAPIDO
(*perking up*)
I know what you mean… I ain't got none of them powers either!

JINX
(*annoyed*)
Let me guess… it's not that they stole the Kraptonite… you're just not entirely sure which one of us was the culprit, am I right?

THE COWL
(*puffing up*)
Correct … one of us - is a thief.

WONDRA
(*musing*)
And a murderer.

BEACON
(*sarcastically*)
A thief and a murderer? Ok, wanna go for the hat trick? How about Arsonist?
Anybody burn anything down lately?

{*there is a pause while they all glare at each other... then RAPIDO starts to put his hand up – WONDRA stomps over to him and he drops it quickly*}

THE COWL
(*playing detective*)
Everyone take a breath. Let's go from the top.

WONDRA
(*crossing her arms*)
One – OMEGAMAN's been murdered.
Two – One of us is responsible.
Three – the only thing that could kill OMEGAMAN was Kraptonite.
Four – One of us stole Kraptonite from Cowl's supposedly theft-proof vault.

RAPIDO
(*chiming in*)
Six – We all had a reason to kill him!
(*they all turn to glare at him... his smile fades*)
Didn't we?

JINX
(*turns to look at WONDRA*)
That's Five, bonehead. But that does bring up an excellent point – Motive.
Why would any of us want OMEGAMAN dead?
Well, I know WONDRA had a good reason, isn't that right, sister?

WONDRA
(*she turns slowly*)
Why on earth would I want to kill OMEGAMAN?

JINX
(*relishing the moment*)
Oh, I don't know…
Maybe because he got tired of pretending that he was in love with a certain well-known TV personality…

THE COWL
(*musing*)
You are saying that he was not in love with LUCY LANNISTER, star report for PNN?

JINX
(*smiling*)
That's right…
The Last Son of Krapton was really in love with… WONDRA!

{*there is a pause – but not the one JINX is looking for… none of the heroes react – JINX looks about all cocksure and proud… but then it fades*}

JINX
(*not understanding*)

Did you hear me?
OMEGAMAN had the hots for WONDRA – he didn't love whats-her-face...
Why isn't this big news?!

THE COWL
(*as if he were pointing out the obvious*)
Because WONDRA is LUCY LANNISTER.

BEACON
(*sighs*)
Yeah, we all knew that...
We only kept up the pretense because "Lucy" always got us primo coverage on the news...

RAPIDO
(*adding his two cents*)
Which led to some pretty sweet endorsement deals...
(*AD MAN voice*)
Hey kids, drink Tempus Fugit™, the high energy drink that keeps going and going and going and going and going and going ... (*until one of the other cast members shuts him up*)!

JINX
(*half to herself, not realizing she is speaking out loud*)
But... but OMEGAMAN was gonna expose that ruse.
He told me he was tired of not being able to be seen in public with the woman he truly loved... so he was gonna blow the lid on the whole Lucy thing...

THE COWL
(*curious*)
Why would he tell you this?

RAPIDO
(*finally has the right answer*)
Because it wasn't really WONDRA he was in love with …
OMEGAMAN was in love… with JINX!

{genuine shock and exclamations from the rest of the CAST – WONDRA loudest of all}

JINX
(*guilty*)
Oh! Heh… well, yeah… I guess.
Hey can I help it the guy had a weakness for these lips?

WONDRA
(*steaming*)
How's about I give you a fat lip, you hussy!

THE COWL
(*to JINX*)
Which gives you an excellent alibi, right?
Perhaps the romance with OMEGAMAN wasn't all it was cracked up to be… either that or you didn't want to share him with the rest of the world.
Everyone knew about his affair with LUCY/WONDRA, so they would naturally expect her – the jilted lover of murdering him!

WONDRA
(*really steamed now*)
You were gonna pin it on me! I'll kill you!

BEACON
(*stepping between them*)

Whoa now... whoa!
Kill her? You've always had a temper WONDRA... and a chip on your shoulder.
Who's to say you didn't kill him for being in love with somebody else?

WONDRA
(*trying to calm down*)

If I was gonna kill him I woulda done it out in the open, in a knock down drag out fight!
And I wouldn't need Kraptonite to do it either!
Yeah, I was upset he was gonna break-up with me, but I had my way of coping...

THE COWL
(*the detective again*)

You had another love interest, someone who's shoulder you could cry on...
Someone close to you, someone you have known for years and years...

{*they all look about for a beat*}

RAPIDO
(*hopeful*)

Wow... I have to admit I'm flattered, but you're really not my type.

BEACON
(*snarky*)

You don't have a type, Ace.
Besides, from what I hear all your love affairs only last a few seconds...

THE COWL
(*musing*)
You were tied of supermen…
You wanted something simple, someone with whom you could be just normal…
(he has positioned himself next to the AUDIENCE MEMBER who plays TIMMY OHLMAN)
Someone like TIMMY OHLMAN!

BEACON
Ohlman!
Cub reporter for PNN

TIMMY OHLMAN
That's right.
I'm the guy who's makin' out with WONDRA tonight!

{*this could play out two ways – depending on the level of attractiveness of the AUDIENCE MEMBER chosen to play TIMMY OHLMAN – WONDRA has been given two sets of lines to choose from*}

WONDRA
(*reacting: positive/negative*)
Slow down there tiger, the night's young! / Uh, let's not be hasty there… Tim.

TIMMY OHLMAN
Oh, don't worry sweetheart (*winks*)
I'm young, virile and my camera's loaded with film!

WONDRA
(*reacting: positive/negative*)

Ho, ho! Tell me more, hot stuff! / Ok there... I don't think we need to hear anymore...

TIMMY OHLMAN

So, hurry up and get this mystery over with so you and I can make "the front page" – if you catch my drift!

WONDRA

(*reacting: positive/negative*)

Ooooh... I love it when you talk all "reporter" to me! / Ah... heh. Yeah, that's... that's kinda not really what I had in mind....

TIMMY OHLMAN

Just tryin' to get things heated up... I'll be waitin' right here, sweetheart!

{*there is a pause after this bit while the others just kind of gape at her - again WONDRA has been given two sets of lines to choose from*}

WONDRA

(*reacting: positive/negative*)

What can I say... he's sooo super hot!! / Let's just kind of say that never happened, ok? Moving on.....

*SFX/MUSIC CUE

{*The CRISIS BEACON flares to life -*

After three blaring tones are heard the SFX will end ...THE COWL presses a button on the SUPERCOMPUTER which plays the V.O. that accompanies this gag/bit}

THE COWL
(*leaping into action, and pressing the button to activate the V.O.*)
This is the Justice Force Crisis Hotline! What is your emergency!

V.O. (*on tape*)
(*ELDERLY CHARACTER VOICE – could be male or female*)
Hello!? Hello!?

BEACON
(*confused*)
Uh … hello? Do you have an emergency?!

V.O. (*on tape*)
Hello!? Hello!?
I don't think anyone is there… Hello?

RAPIDO
(*smiling*)
Sounds just like my Grandma/Grandpa! Hey Mee-Maw/Pap-pap!

V.O. (*on tape*)
Is this thing working… all I'm hearing is some gol durn static!
Hello! Hello!

JINX
(*getting steamed*)
LISTEN UP YOU OLD FART/BAT! THIS IS AN EMERGENCY HOTLINE
STATE YOUR EMERGENCY!?

V.O. (*on tape*)

I'm gonna call the Better Business Bureau on you! Roto-rooter my ass!

{In disgust, THE COWL snaps off the V.O. The heroes all look at each other for a beat}

WONDRA
(*scowling at COWL*)
Still haven't managed to get that thing fixed, huh, techno-wiz?

BEACON
(*backtracking*)
I'm a bit confused – what we were talking about before –
That whole OMEGAMAN loves-me-he-loves-me-not thing
Did we actually establish a motive for anyone in all of that?

THE COWL
(*shrugging*)
Not really – it's was all a red herring to mislead and confuse and also work in another Audience Member… Part of our comedy mystery contractual obligations….

{the cast members congratulate each and give high-fives, "good job!" etc. – then back to business}

THE COWL
(*analyzing*)
But let's go over a few bits of our history with OMEGAMAN…
At one time or another, each of us has had a grudge against him, correct?
(*counts off on his fingers – each cast member reacts to his accusation*)
JINX – your father The Great Zoltan was one of the first villain's OMEGAMAN fought.

OMEGAMAN sent him away to prison for years and it drove your father insane. Your motive is Revenge.

JINX
(*defensive*)
So?! My father was misguided, and he went mad because of OMEGAMAN – and I had to work extra hard to be accepted as a member of the Justice Force and try to clear my father's name! I coulda killed him for that!

THE COWL
(*moving on*)
BEACON – you were extremely angry that OMEGAMAN had topped your previously unbeaten high score in the televised Battle of the Network Superstars. Your motive is Pride.

BEACON
(*defensive*)
Stupid cheater! He won on a technicality; I shoulda been the winner I tell yeah! Do you know how many 'nyah nyah nyah' letters I got because of that! I coulda killed him for that!

THE COWL
(*moving on*)
WONDRA – you were pretty burned up by OMEGAMAN's affection for your alter-ego – envious of the other woman, even though the other woman was you! Your motive is Jealousy!

WONDRA
(*defensive*)
I got so tired of the on again/off again thing – it's so high school! I'm a grown woman, I got needs!! I coulda killed him for that!

THE COWL
(*moving on*)
RAPIDO – you blamed OMEGAMAN for the industrial waste accident that affected your super speed – if I remember correctly it dropped your speed ranking from #1 to #33. Ouch.
Your motive is Humiliation.

RAPIDO
(*defensive*)
Yeah! That big dumb jerk caused that accident – I spent six months on the "disabled" list because he "accidently" knocked that tanker of waste over! I coulda killed him for that!
But what about you? You had a beef with him too, right?

JINX
(*jumping in*)
You bet your sweet bippy he did!
Every one of us knows how many times OMEGAMAN over ruled you at the Justice Force meetings –We all know how much you want to be leader of the Justice Force! Gloom and Doom here's got a Little Brother Complex! His motive is Control!

THE COWL
(*snarling*)
I'll admit that I did have issue with how he ran the Justice Force - that and the noogies he used to give me in the locker room – I really hated that guy sometimes – but I am not the killer!

WONDRA
(*haughty*)
Yeah? Prove it!
You just admitted you hated the guy!

THE COWL
(*countering*)
You yourself pointed out that you wouldn't have used Kraptonite against OMEGAMAN – preferring instead to pummel him with your fists. Much the same way, I would've used my superior intellect to kill him – I've already computed half a dozen ways to do that very thing – but none of the scenarios I had come up with resulted in his actual death – someone beat me to the punch!

BEACON
(*flippant*)
Yeah, well ... I just would've just blasted him with cosmic rays from my power ring.

THE COWL
(*picking up on that*)
Precisely! Your Power Ring has the ability to use the myriad types of cosmic radiation in order for you to overpower your foes ... Tell us, Bacon... what setting is your ring currently on?

BEACON
(*irritated*)
It's BEACON! Loosen that darn headgear of yours, will ya!
(*looking at his ring*)
My ring is set to ... Holy Moly! Kraptonite!

THE COWL
(*big reveal*)
A-ha! Listen up, Justice Force – each of us will find that we all have some element or particles of Kraptonite on our person.

{*COWL steps over to the SUPERCOMPUTER and fiddles with the dials*}

JINX
(*this is giving her a headache*)
How the heck do you know that!?

THE COWL
(*smugly*)
From the moment we stepped into the Hall of Freedom, each of us has been scanned by the Justice Force Security and Defense Systems. All of the information gathered has been analyzed, catalogued and distilled to reveal threats to our safety – including any trace of Kraptonite!
(*pointing at BEACON*) A power ring set to Kraptonite radiation!
(*pointing at WONDRA*) Amazonian Passion Perfume – laced with Kraptonite molecules!
(*pointing at RAPIDO*) The soles of your Friction Tread Boots contain slivers of Kraptonite!
(*pointing at JINX*) And your wand has been coated in a fine radioactive dust - Kraptonite dust!

{*the others are stunned and react to these revelations*}

RAPIDO
(*distressed*)
Yeah … well, what about you pal? I bet you got some Kraptonite on you too… is that right?

THE COWL
(*nodding in agreement*)
All of my equipment is monitored and maintained by nanobot technology – and all of the nanobots have been laced with Kraptonite particles!

RAPIDO
(*amazed*)
Holy Tiny Terrors!

JINX
(*getting back to the point*)
Alright, now we're getting somewhere – each of us has a motive and each of us had the means…
What about opportunity?

BEACON
(*clearing his throat*)
Well, I think that…

WONDRA
(*stepping to the fore*)
I got this sister…

BEACON
(*reacting*)
Hey!

{*the others giggle*}

WONDRA
Well, my perfume was somehow mysteriously laced with Kraptoinite –
OMEGAMAN was standing pretty close to me during that battle –
He could've inhaled the poisoned perfume – a few inhales and BAM! one dead Kraptonian…

{*all of the character's look about, agreeing with her analysis*}

                        WONDRA
                    (*goes down the line*)
THE COWL was using his nanobots to infiltrate Rex's robots with
         a virus in order to disrupt their programming –
     Robots OMEGAMAN was tearing apart with his hands –
    Thus exposing him to the fatal Kraptonite gas of the nanobots…

{all of the character's look about, agreeing with her analysis}

                        WONDRA
                     (*on to the next*)
     BEACON's ring was somehow mistakenly tuned to Kraptonite
       radiation and those beams were crisscrossing the battlefield –
      And OMEGAMAN flew through them time and time again –
             Soaking up the deadly Kraptonite energy…

{all of the character's look about, agreeing with her analysis}

                        WONDRA
                      (*and the next*)
            JINX's wand was covered in Kraptonite dust –
   Which fused with her magic spells, turning them into Kraptoinite
                        laced death beams!

{all of the character's look about, agreeing with her analysis}

                        WONDRA
                    (*and finally RAPIDO*)
    And Speedy Gonzales here was whipping all around the place –
        one of those slivers could've been directed straight into
    OMEGAMAN's mouth unseen, undetected and unstoppable – the
  result, OMEGAMAN choking to death on a tiny sliver of turquoise
                             doom!

{there is a beat while all the characters take all of this in, and then they break out in applause, congratulating WONDRA on her performance}

THE COWL
(*with admiration*)
An excellent analysis, WONDRA…

BEACON
(*miffed*)
Yeah, well… I was gonna say all of that…

JINX
(*getting on with it*)
Ok – we've each got a motive, we've each got the means and we each had the opportunity…
Now what?

RAPIDO
(*rubbing his tummy*)
Lunch? Anybody else hungry?

JINX
(*whirling on him*)
I'm so gonna cast a shut the hell up spell on you…

THE COWL
(*thinking*)
Hhhhhhmmmm. Well, we all do seem to have means, motive and opportunity. But perhaps we're missing some important clues or pieces of evidence… something that will reveal who the real murderer is.

I say we call upon these folks here who have been watching to help us out.

Okay, folks here's your chance to play detective . . . you get the chance to ask each of us suspects a couple a questions about the untimely death of OMEGAMAN. Let's start the questioning with --WONDRA.

(*pause*)

Any questions for our other lovely female champion, JINX?

(*pause*)

How about BEACON, any questions for him?

(*pause*)

How about RAPIDO, any questions for him?

(*pause*)

And last but not least, myself, does anyone have any questions for me?

Okay folks, now that the questioning is over with, it's time for you to solve this mystery. Find that sheet of paper inside your program marked Detective Sheet.

Now here's how to fill them out:

Write down the name of the person whom you think killed OMEGAMAN.

Then write down why, and be as specific as possible, because the one who comes closest to the right answers gonna win some nice prizes, okay? After that, if you would all be so kind as to flip the sheet over and fill out the little questionnaire on the back, we'd appreciate it.

If you want to know about upcoming shows we might be having, please be sure to include your address and zip code and we'll add you to our mailing list. That'll help us to keep bringing you more quality, educational programming like this for years to come!

And most important of all, don't forget to sign your name… you can't win a prize if we don't know the name of the person who won it!

We'll be back to collect those sheets in a few moments.

END
ACT ONE

ACT TWO

{The top of Act Two begins (**Rule of Three – it's always Funny Three times**) when the CRISIS BEACON begins to twirl and flash and the SFX of the CRISIS ALERT is head over the speakers. The lights should come up as the entire cast – BEACON, COWL, JINX, RAPIDO and WONDRA jog into the room – COWL moves up to the SUPERCOMPUTER and pushes a few buttons and silences the alarm (it can be queued to fade or be cut off from off stage) the others wait for a beat while COWL continues to futz with the SUPERCOMPUTER}

***SFX/MUSIC CUE**

THE COWL
(leaping into action, and pressing the button to activate the V.O.)
You've reached the Justice Force Crisis Hotline! What is your emergency!

V.O. *(on tape)*
(STONER VOICE)
Yo! Mikey – is that you!?
Mikey – it's Joey!

WONDRA
(barely restraining her anger)
Seriously – does everyone have this frickin' number!?!

V.O. *(on tape)*
Yo – Mikey!
We soooo got the munchies, dude!
Hook us up with some Zaa, bro!

JINX
(*dumbfounded*)
This. Is. Not. A Pizza Joint! We are the Justice Force – a cadre of elite superheroes who save the world on a daily basis – not deliver pizza to a bunch of slackwit nutjobs sitting in their apartment playing video games!

V.O. (*on tape*)
Whoa – How did you know we were playing video games… dude… that is spooky!

THE COWL
(*perturbed*)
You have the wrong number – goodbye!

V.O. (*on tape*)
Wait! Wait! We need breadsticks, dude! Breadsticks!

{*In disgust, THE COWL snaps off the V.O. The heroes all look at each other for a beat*}

WONDRA
(*crossing her arms*)
We should so switch to T-Mobile.

THE COWL
(*taking charge*)
All right – enough funny business! It's time to bring OMEGAMAN's killer to Justice!

{*there is a beat – the others look at COWL*}

BEACON
(*smirking*)
You did that just to strike the hero pose, didn't you?

JINX
(*miffed*)
Will you guys get serious! Look, we know it was one of us – we know that one of us used Kraptonite to kill OMEGAMAN and we all know each of us has a motive… the heroic thing to do would be to fess up!

{*there is a beat – the others look around, no one wanting to admit to being the killer*}

JINX
(*sighing, frustrated*)
Oh, come on guys – look, we don't know how much time we have until a real crisis happens – if we don't figure this out we're going to be out of time!

THE COWL
(*snapping his fingers*)
An excellent observation JINX!
This whole mystery hinges on Time!

BEACON
(*confused*)
Really? How so?

THE COWL
(*detective*)

The key to this whole mystery is the Kraptonite – not the material itself, but rather how each of us came to possess the deadly substance that killed OMEGAMAN.
It's true that separately, each of us could've secured the Kraptonite and found a way to use it against him...
However – only one of us had the time to ensure that the turquoise tincture of turpitude we each carried would be unwittingly used against OMEGAMAN – only one of us had a grudge that they had been carrying all this Time – and only one of us has all the Time in the world...
Isn't that right --- RAPIDO!

{a moment of shock as the CAST gasps in surprise}

RAPIDO
(*shrugs*)
Hey, well... you got me!
Yeah -- I made sure that big stupid goody-goody got his!
(*he looks about at the others with a villainous glare*)
Do you know how embarrassing it was to have my face plastered all over the tabloids?
Speedy's Lost his Zip! - Just a Flash in the Pan! - World's Fastest – Not!
So yeah, I zipped into THE COWL Cave when you had the vault open, zoomed past before you could see me, snagged the Kraptonite and made sure I was able to plant it on all of you without you knowing... (*snaps his fingers*)
Kraptonite dust all over JINX's wand... (*snaps his fingers*)
Kraptonite particles inside WONDRA's perfume bottle ... (*snaps his fingers*)
Bim Bam Boom, Kraptonite molecules all up in your nanobots grill! (*snaps his fingers*)

And what kind of doofus has a power ring with a setting for deadly radiation –
(*he glares at BEACON and gives him a double-snap*) oh yeah … Bacon does.
And it was so easy to flick (*makes a flicking gesture*) that little sliver of Kraptonite down that big jerk's throat… since he always had his big fat mouth open!

JINX
(*ready for a fight*)
You dusted my wand!? I'll murderize ya!

WONDRA
(*super pissed*)
You tainted my Tommy Girl!? Get ready for a boot stompin' Quickie-McQuickerson!

THE COWL
(*analyzing*)
Beating my security system is going to cost you, jerk-face!

BEACON
(*sheepish*)
Funny thing is… my ring really isn't source of power – it's the boots actually. Power Boots.

{*there is a beat – the others look at BEACON*}

BEACON
(*dropping the ruse*)
Just kidding – yeah it's the Ring!
And for tampering with the Power Cosmic – prepare to get blasted in the next Dimension, pal!

RAPIDO
(*laughs*)
You guys just don't get it!
World's Fastest Human! Ppffft! You're never gonna catch me!

{*RAPIDO makes a quick move and assumes a RUNNING POSE - the gag here is that he thinks he is running at SUPERSPEED, but the combined powers of the others – JINX uses her wand, COWL uses his Cowl Gun, BEACON uses his Power Ring and WONDRA uses her Amazonian Lasso – the combination of which will have him frozen in place*}

JINX, THE COWL, WONDRA, and BEACON
(*all together*)
Zhasam! Blammo! Ka-pow! Yippie-K-Y-Sucka!

RAPIDO
(*thinks he miles away by now*)
Those morons probably think I'm still in the room…!

BEACON
(*he goes up to RAPIDO and pokes him in the head*)
That is too wild! He can't see, hear or feel anything can he?!

JINX
(*to the others*)
Numbskull thinks he's moving at hyper-speed…
In reality he's been trapped in his own speed zone… and our combined power output should keep him there for, oh, the next 600 years or so!

WONDRA
(*proudly*)
Yep…
Hey, maybe we can use him as like a coat rack or something!

THE COWL
(*agreeing*)
We do need a place for visitors to hang their capes…

JINX
(*gloating*)
He's totally going to get decorated at Christmas time…

*SFX/MUSIC CUE

{*The CRISIS BEACON flares to life -*

After three blaring tones are heard the SFX will end …THE COWL presses a button on the SUPERCOMPUTER which plays the V.O. that accompanies this gag/bit}

THE COWL
(*leaping into action, and pressing the button to activate the V.O.*)
This is the Justice Force Crisis Hotline! What is your emergency!

V.O. (*on tape*)
(*a gruff male voice*)
Justice Force! This is Warden Jones – Rex Ruthless has escaped from prison and he's says he's going to destroy the world… in Four Minutes!

WONDRA
(*leaping into action, and pressing the button to activate the V.O.*)

Four Minutes – C'mon gang – we got ourselves some world saving to do!!

{all EXIT heroically as Madonna's "4 Minutes" plays}
"4 Minutes"
(feat. Justin Timberlake, Timbaland)

{there is a beat – after the applause and the music fades}

RAPIDO
(still frozen in place)
Guys?! Guys! Hey – you gotta let me outta here – c'mon man… I gotta pee!

THE END?

David J. Fielding has worn many hats in his brief time upon this globe - among them the actor who played Zordon on the *Mighty Morphin' Power Rangers* television series, and voice actor for video games such as **Empire Earth, Dungeon Siege: Legends of Aranna, Zeus, Poseidon,** and **Anvil of Dawn.** He is an accomplished actor and comedian and performs regularly with Player One an improv troupe in Pittsburgh that performs at the Arcade Comedy Theater and acting and writing with **Mystery's Most Wanted** a popular murder mystery dinner theater troupe in Pittsburgh, PA. He has three decades of stage and film experience as well as numerous stage roles including roles such as Saleri in *Amadeus* and Quentin in *After the Fall.* David holds two degrees in acting, a BFA from Southwest Texas State and an MFA from the University of Pittsburgh. He is busy working on his superhero novel and several short stories and a number of other murder mystery plays.

Made in the USA
Lexington, KY
09 July 2013